# BAPTIZED ATHEIST

# BAPTIZED ATHEIST

## DAVID SMALLEY

Foreword by Dr. David Eller

2010
American Atheist Press
Cranford, New Jersey

ISBN-13:978-1-57884-008-3
ISBN-10: 1-57884-008-2

American Atheist Press
P.O. Box 5733
Parsippany, NJ 07054-6733

www.atheists.org

Edited by Frank R. Zindler & Dr. David Eller

**Library of Congress Cataloging-in-Publication Data**

Smalley, David, 1980-
Baptized atheist / David Smalley ; foreword by David Eller.
  p. cm.
Includes bibliographical references.
ISBN 978-1-57884-008-3 (alk. paper)
1. Smalley, David, 1980- 2. Christianity and atheism. 3.
Atheists--United States--Biography. 4. Ex-church members--
United States--Biography. I. Title.
  BL2790.S57A3 2010
  261.2'1092--dc22
  [B]
                                         2010020053

# CONTENTS

# FOREWORD
Dr. David Eller

The three major proselytizing religions have one interesting and important thing in common: they all center on the life of an individual. Buddhism has its Siddhartha, Christianity its Jesus, Islam its Muhammad. Each religion is thus first and foremost the chronicle of a person—his successes and failures, his teachings and actions, the stories that he told and the story that he lived. In some religions, the key actors are deities, like Krishna in Hinduism, and traditional or tribal religions are rich in personal figures like Zeus, Odin, Osiris, and many more—all with their personalities, their mates, their offspring, and their various adventures (not always good or beneficent or moral).

Whatever beliefs or doctrines or dogmas may comprise religions—religions are never beliefs or doctrines or dogmas alone, and they never can be. Those things are too abstract, too bloodless, too literal. Humans need stories; humans are the species that does and must tell stories. This is why at the heart of all religion stands a great story that is more than a sequence of events. It is a narrative, that is, a developing and unfolding tale that goes somewhere, that has some unifying trajectory and theme. All of the particular events in the story point to something and contribute to the message of, the reason for, the story and the journey undertaken in it.

These stories have another function as well. They not only describe some character in the past; they also point a way to a future. They tell us how we should act and live. They become the foundation of the ideas and institutions of today and set a precedent for tomorrow. Think specifically of Christianity: many

Christians believe that certain arrangements (say, heterosexual marriage or the different languages in the world) are the result of founding actions in the past, and many use the person of Jesus to determine what they should do today (sometimes consciously asking "What would Jesus do?"). For Muslims, the perfect person is Muhammad, and they organize their lives around his sayings and doings; he is the lawgiver and model. For Buddhists, the first Buddha is the great teacher and paragon. In all religions, the beliefs are less important than the behaviors of the individuals who came before us. Our duty as modern mortal beings is to follow in their footsteps. Members of religions are thus not so much *believers* as *followers*.

All of the great stories—the ones that resonate with us, the ones that we continue to tell and retell for years, generations, millennia—have the same basic form. They are accounts of struggles, of travels and trials, of ordeals undertaken and lessons learned. They are fundamentally and universally tales of transformation: we begin the journey in one condition and end it in another.

For the nature of any powerful and persistent story is the quest. It may be a quest after a monster or a maiden, an artifact or an answer. But whatever the goal, the story reports a pursuit, and three things about this pursuit are essential: the thing pursued is valuable or "true," the pursuer is courageous and heroic because the pursuit is dangerous or even deadly, and the pursuing hero emerges changed—not always victorious but always improved.

There is only one small difference between the story and the biography: the biography is supposedly the story of a real person in recent time. David Smalley has offered us in the book you are about to read his own personal quest which is as heroic as any Hercules, Odysseus, or Beowulf. Smalley was brave to start the journey he recounts, and he is twice brave to recount it. Like any hero of lore, he faces many tests and challenges along the way. Many figures try to dissuade him from his path: they tell him that he is a fool, that he is wrong, that he will be punished, that he will fail. But, like any mythical hero, he persists. Occasionally he stumbles. But he is in pursuit of something precious, and he will not be denied.

The first brave act of any search is to realize that there is something to search for, to realize some lack. Religions typically claim that there is no lack at all: Tertullian, the early Christian church father, asserted that the believer's first belief is that there is nothing else to believe but the belief. But such a person does not go on quests; he sits at home, confident that he has all that he needs. For such a person, there is no valor and there is no story. At best, he lives out someone else's story.

David Smalley's story is not anyone else's. Many of us have had experiences similar to his, but he is not following us. He intrepidly steps off onto a path alone, even against the counsel and pressure of his initial comrades. He finds friends and allies along the way, as all heroes do. He takes strength and guidance from his friends, but the quest is his own. No one can take your journey for you, and he understood that before he began.

Like a good hero, Smalley maintains his humor even as he nears his goal. But, happily, unlike many a tragic hero, he does reach his destination and lives to tell; his quest is fulfilled. Two things are true in the end. First, he is a transformed person when he completes his adventure—better and freer than he started. Second, like any memorable story, his offers a model for others to emulate, that they too may be free. No one—not Smalley, not myself—expects or commands others to follow him, to take the path he took and reach the shore he reached. But each of us can and must take our own journey, go on our own search, undertake our own quest, or else we are merely living someone else's life.

# CHAPTER 1: SKEPTICISM

# I WANTED TO BELIEVE

I'd like to tell you I was raised as a Christian, but in fact, like most Americans, I was raised in a theistic household that *thought* we were Christians. I can't blame my mother; she just didn't know the difference. She honestly thought a fear of 'God' and a decent life style meant that she was doing the best for her children. Considering the childhood she had, mine was a picnic! I rarely needed anything I didn't have, and while much of my childhood was technically below the poverty line for income levels, I never knew it. I had a happy, wonderful childhood. The assumption in my family was that as long as we didn't do anything too terribly bad, and maintained our belief in Jesus, and 'God' as his father, we wouldn't go to Hell. I was okay with that. And so it was.

Christianity just isn't that cut and dried, and the term is used too loosely, which I will get into a little later. As a teenager, I began playing drums for different musical groups ranging from rock to country-western (just because I loved playing) and finally found solace in playing for local gospel choirs. I wasn't metaphysically inspired by any means; I just gravitated towards the funk and blues-oriented style of music. Not to mention, I was often a local celebrity as the "little white kid" playing drums professionally for an all-black church, and it was a blast.

I joined several Baptist churches as a drummer, and that allowed me to see the way many religious organizations operate from the inside. I witnessed some unspeakable acts of deceit and manipulation from self-proclaimed 'Men of God.' However, I stayed the course, not to let mere humans deter me from my personal relationship with 'God.'

One day, at sixteen years old, I finally decided to take that leap of faith and become baptized. Looking back, I never really began to understand what it meant to be Christian until that day. As the crowd of sixty looked on, I stood in the warm 'holy water' at the First Baptist Church of Everman, in a small town in Texas, and Pastor Mike said to me, *"Do you believe Jesus Christ died for your sins so that you may enter the Kingdom of Heaven?"* I nervously responded, *"Yes."* He continued, *"Then you are hereby saved in the name of the Father, the Son, and the Holy Spirit."*

As the water covered my ears and face, and my breathing paused, I briefly questioned my answer. I thought to myself, *"I think I believe in God, but how could one man's death result in the salvation of billions, and how does killing the innocent pardon the guilty?"* This just didn't make sense to me, and I was puzzled. Upon breaking the surface of the water, I continued to ponder the agreement I had just made. It was surreal. I was walking up the steps out of the baptistery, draped in a pure white gown, soaked from head to toe, as water was dripping with each step. The crowd was cheering, but I had never been more confused in my entire life. What had I just accomplished? I thought to myself, *"Why should that tragedy of Jesus' death have to take place if God were in control? Why would a righteous god demand the blood, torture and death of anyone, let alone his only son?"* Most importantly, I thought *"Why haven't I thought about this before now?! What have I done?!*

These are typical questions to have regarding your faith and are valid to ask. I suppose I had just gone along with everyone else because I thought it was part of life, and I had always been taught that if you ever said you *weren't* Christian, then you were immediately 'bad.' Getting baptized was just something boys did, like going to school, and shaving for the first time. I never really thought about it with a free and opened mind before. The pastor had just asked me that question in front of the entire congregation, and it felt so official, that I really started to think about my answer for the first time in my life.

As others were being baptized, and the ceremony was being completed, I realized the pastor must have seen the doubt on my face. He leaned close to me and lightly said, *"You know, son, you can't just say you believe; you have to know it to be true in your heart."* At that very moment, I realized I did not fully believe, and I could no longer lie to myself and pretend to be something I did not understand. I did not feel it in my heart. I didn't even know what that meant, for the heart cannot actually feel emotions. I had so many logical questions that just couldn't be explained away with faith. I needed answers and immediately regretted my commitment to Christ. Not so much because I wanted to turn away from Christianity, but I just felt that I had made a commitment that I was not yet ready for. It should have been an educated decision, and I was not yet educated on the topic.

Even after my strange baptism and newfound skepticism for Christianity, I stayed with the church. Remember, I was also an important part of the choir and attended with a few friends from school. I couldn't exactly just turn my back on the church because

I had a few questions. I had effectively become a part of the group, and in turn, the group was a part of me.

My ingrained belief was so strong that, even though I had doubts, I pushed them away and continued to speak of 'God,' 'Heaven,' and 'angels,' as though they were as real as you and I, without knowing what those words actually meant. I said "bless you" when people sneezed, although I didn't quite understand what was blessing them (as if I had that power). Essentially, I thought there was something very wrong with me for even doubting my faith, and I wanted to be a better Christian. I was now riddled with guilt, and had a lot of work to do.

As I walked around the community with our youth group, knocking on doors to tell people about Jesus, I often thought: *"These people have their own faith, and some have none at all; how do I know I have it right?"* For all I knew, maybe *they* had it figured out, and I was the one going to Hell. What if the Baptists were wrong? What if my preacher was wrong? After all, he was just a man.

With enormous questions in front of me, I set out on a personal journey to find the truth. The real truth—not what people *told* me was true. Each and every religion on the planet claims to have the truth and likely has very good evidence pointing to that fact. Why is that? This is our eternity we're talking about! I didn't want to be convinced of how to live and die based on a good sales pitch, or threats of eternal punishment. I wanted to make an educated decision and see what was really going on in the world of religion in *all aspects*, not just what I knew to be in my world or in the specific Bible verses my preacher chose to make a point. Moreover, I didn't want to be as arrogant as to think that only American Baptist Christians had it right, and everyone else was just wrong because they didn't 'have Jesus,' without actually looking into what others believe.

Two things were for sure: I had doubts around the existence of 'God' that I didn't want to admit, and if this god did exist, I wanted to be sure I was living and worshipping in the most effective way that resulted in me going to Heaven. Basically, because I didn't want to make any mistakes, I started approaching religion with logical reason instead of blind faith. I began asking questions...

## THE SON OR THE GOD?

I wasn't quite brave enough to question a preacher just yet, but I took an opportunity while talking with a Pentecostal friend of mine, who was deeply involved with his religion, to squeeze in a bit of skepticism. I openly asked him, *"Is Jesus the same person as God, or is he God's son?"* He quickly walked me out to his car where he kept a Bible, eager to proselytize.

We flipped through the pages, bouncing from verse to verse, as he proved to me that Jesus was no doubt the son of the Christian god, Yahweh. He pointed to specific scriptures to prove his point. I walked away from the car with an understanding, that Jesus and 'God' were two separate entities, Jesus being the offspring, and Yahweh, the father.

Armed with this new information, I engaged my new preacher in casual conversation and braggingly mentioned what I had discovered. He almost seemed offended as he rushed me into his office and asked me to have a seat.

He proceeded to flip through the very same version of the Bible where I found my original information and ultimately proved to me that my Pentecostal friend was misguided, and in fact, Jesus and 'God' were one in the same. He pointed to Colossians 2:9, where Paul is describing Jesus and declares; *"In Him dwells all the fullness of the Godhead, bodily."* He also described the Trinity, in which the spirit of 'God' is in three forms, "the Father, the Son, and the Holy Spirit." He likened that to me being both a son and a brother, yet I am one person. While I agreed that his biblical points were convincing, I just didn't follow his logic. Although I could hold two titles at once, we were talking about the relationships to two different people. I am the son to my *mother* and a brother to my *sisters*, but I couldn't be both to either of them, and Jesus couldn't be the father and that father's son at the same time—at least not without throwing logic out the window.

My preacher may have walked away from the meeting feeling victorious over my Pentecostal friend, but in reality I was beginning to lose trust in the Bible as a credible source of information. I was only one question into my journey, and I had already discovered that the Bible is a subjective book. It is left up to our own interpretation—like a wild card used to fit any lifestyle one chooses.

This explains the many denominations of Christianity, but how could we ever know who was *really* right? The credibility of religious leaders doesn't play a role, because there are wealthy, educated scholars at the top of every major religious denomination, all claiming to be the 'truth.' But how could they all consider themselves to be 'Christians,' when they disagree on basic fundamental properties of 'Christ?'

So, who was Jesus really? I heard of him as the Messiah and the 'Son of God,' but his life and origins were very mysterious to most around me that considered themselves Christian. I took a brief moment of my journey to research the attributes of the most important figure in Christianity's history. After all, if I was going to worship and be the best Christian possible, I needed a solid understanding of whom I was following.

I began searching for topics such as *Messiah, miracle worker,* and *healer.* I also looked into the history of Roman crucifixions.

One name always seemed to accompany Jesus' in my findings. The name was Apollonius of Tyana. He was essentially a Greek philosopher, whose followers claimed he had the powers to heal, walk through walls, raise the dead, and perform various other miracles. He was persecuted for his religious beliefs by the Romans and was crucified in a similar manner as is told of Jesus' death. The most amazing part of this is that Apollonius' story doesn't end there. He allegedly died on a cross, after which he ascended to Heaven and came back, appearing to his followers. This was no impersonator of Jesus. He is said to have lived at the exact same time as Jesus, but with far less popularity.

So here's the basic history: the Orthodox Jews had compiled the Tanakh as their holy book, (which is basically the Old Testament of the Christian Bible). In that book, as you can read today, it speaks of a Messiah coming to earth one day as the son of 'God.' Apollonius of Tyana claimed to be that Messiah. Many men claimed to be that Messiah, and each of them was refused by the Jews. That's why when Jesus came with the same message; the Jews also turned him away—just as they do today. In the 1970's, Jim Jones also claimed to be the Messiah, but was considered a cult leader who led the Jonestown Massacre of over 900 innocent people. David Koresh suffered the same fate in the '90s. Cults are constantly popping up all over the world, with the leader claiming to be the human embodiment of a 'Lord.' So why do so many people willingly follow Jesus?

Once I found names like Jesus and Apollonius being linked together, it led to an astounding discovery. I learned of a mystical god named Horus, who was said to be the son of another god,

Osiris. In an Egyptian myth, Horus was quoted as saying "I and my Father are one." While this bears a striking resemblance to Jesus and Yahweh, I couldn't ignore the following facts. Osiris' birth was announced by three wise men, and he was referred to as the Lord of Lords, Kings of Kings, God of Gods, and was the resurrection and the Life, the Good Shepherd, and Everlastingness. To the Egyptians, Osiris was the god that came in human form and suffered for them. He also rose after his death. His son, Horus, was born on December 25th, to a virgin in a cave. He later had twelve disciples and was baptized by 'Anup the Baptizer' much like 'John the Baptist.' He walked on water and was called the *KRST*, or 'anointed one.' This story predates Christianity by more than 1500 years.

Shocked at this new evidence, I continued searching for other similar stories. It didn't take long to discover a god named Dionysus. He too was born of a virgin, called the 'Holy Child,' performed miracles, and rose from the dead in late March.

Another god by the name of Attis of Phrygia was also born to a virgin named Nana. He was considered the savior and said that his body was bread, to be eaten by his worshippers. He was both the Divine Son and the Father. He was crucified on a tree, from which his holy blood ran down to redeem the earth. He then descended into the underworld—and three days later resurrected on March 25th as the "Most High God."

Finally, a god who is still very popular today is the Hindu god Krishna. Hinduism is primarily practiced in modern-day India. Krishna was born to the virgin Devaki (Devine One) on (you guessed it) December 25th. His father was a carpenter, and a star in the east signaled his birth. He worked miracles and wonders, raising the dead and healing the deaf and the blind. He used parables to teach people about love and charity, and he lived in voluntary poverty. Krishna had a beloved disciple named Ar-jouan, very close to the modern name of John. He was killed around the age of 30 but rose from the dead and ascended to Heaven in the "sight of all men." He was deemed the 'Son of God' and specifically died as the savior of all mankind. Krishna's disciples noted him as being called the Redeemer and gave him the title of 'Jezeus' and 'Jeseus' which means 'pure essence.'

Even if we are able to get beyond the confusing notion of the Trinity within Christianity, we must challenge the entire topic of sacrifice. If I were to sacrifice something, that means I lose it—giving it up for a cause or purpose I deemed necessary. But the Christian belief is that Jesus is with 'the Father' right now—alive and well in Heaven. So what did the father *really* sacrifice? He still has his son! If 'God' and Jesus are one in the same, then they both know 'all.' That means they knew Jesus would be killed, they knew he would be resurrected three days later, and they knew he would ascend back to Heaven so they could be together. Other than a few days of whipping, and the pain of palm-damage done to his human flesh, I'm having a hard time seeing what was actually sacrificed. If I let you stay in my home for a week and then kicked you out so I could move back in, I could hardly take credit for 'sacrificing' my house to you! It just seems like the whole thing was more of a planned temporary displacement than a sacrifice. The stories even refer to Jesus as the "sacrificial lamb," but every other lamb that was sacrificed is still dead. According to

Christianity, Jesus is not. Again, where is the sacrifice? At this point, I was really struggling with one of the major components of Christianity and doubted a very critical portion of its foundation.

After all, on the surface, it certainly didn't make sense that a god would be so unhappy with his creation, and then feel he could repair things by impregnating a virgin with himself, so that the people of his creation could sacrifice him back to himself as atonement for *their* behavior.

We'd like to think that the story of Jesus is an original truth, and comes with an unexpected and amazing feat of sacrifice, but the facts above are very real and caused me to take a deep look into the history behind Christian beliefs. Perhaps I could find the necessary proof and do the world a favor by proving that Christianity was the truth.

## EXAMINING THE BIBLE

With my new responsibility of changing the world, I wanted to arm myself with the best knowledge possible on Christianity. What better place to begin than the Holy Bible? I decided I would read it cover to cover, have my questions answered, and then tell the world the good news.

So I went to a quiet room with my bottle of water and got comfortable. With the Bible in my lap, I admit that I was deeply intimidated by this enormous book. I opened it and began reading.

"In the beginning, God created the Heavens and the earth." That seemed simple enough; but how? I was amazed by the details that followed. On the first day, the world was created and 'God' separated the darkness from the light, calling the darkness 'night' and the light, he called 'day.' Then, it went on to tell me about the second day, but I immediately paused. He is 'God,' why was that all he could do in a day? This already didn't make sense to me. I thought, "Why would he be limited, or perhaps limit himself to only accomplishing two things in a single day...and how long could that have really taken God?" I was slightly confused, but I went on.

On the second day, he divided the waters horizontally, calling the top portion "Heaven." Okay, this one really didn't compute. I supposed that the blue sky above appeared the same as water to this ancient writer; and for the first time, I began to see a human influence in the *good* book. Of course today, we know that water isn't hovering above the land and that water suspended above us isn't the reason our sky is blue. I still continued reading.

On the third day, he demanded that dry land appear and created grass, trees, plants, and fruits. On day four, he created the sun and the moon. My eyes stopped reading as I stared at the words in front of me. I was nearly frozen in confusion. I said aloud to myself, *"It's the fourth day—and we're just now getting the sun?"* I went back to the beginning and searched over each verse, and sure enough, each day of creation ended with *"the evening and the morning"* being the signs of the completion of that day. I thought to myself, *"How did he have an evening and a morning three times in a row, with no sun or moon?"* I laid my head back in the comfortable chair and said aloud, *"How were plants and trees here a full day before the sun, when the sun is necessary for survival of vegetation?"* I was only a few verses into the first chapter of Genesis, and I wasn't buying it. I didn't see how any intelligent adult who understood science even in the slightest, could. I continued on.

The fifth day began the life in the oceans, and in the air, as Jehovah created all the fishes, sea life, and birds. On the sixth day, he created man. Although I was a bit confused, at least I now understood the creation order and the Christian viewpoint of how the earth and life on earth began. But there was no way I could defend that ridiculous account of events without more evidence! So I continued reading.

I made it all the way to the second chapter of Genesis, and the fourth verse hit me like a ton of bricks—yet another creation story! In this version, the earth was not a formless void but a vast desert, without water. The second astonishing mention was that man was created first—apparently to till the land. Only after this

was the creation of the Garden of Eden, animals, and eventually a woman when no mate was found suitable for man.

I began to understand at this point in my journey, why so many Christians say that all questions will be answered in the end. If you go through the Bible trying to make it all make sense, you will fail. At some point, you will either make up your mind that it doesn't, but choose to trust it anyway with faith—or you will inspect it as an investigator and find so many holes in the logic that you will no longer believe it at all. I had a feeling I was treading toward the latter direction, and that terrified me. I wanted so bad to believe, I just couldn't wrap my head around this nonsense.

I was unable to defend the Bible's logic; but was that because of my ignorance? Could I turn things around? Surely I just needed more information. So many people I knew and respected were Christians, and I was absolutely sure they knew of these problems within the book. I knew that millions of people had accepted these stories as true yet still followed Christianity and trusted the Bible as the 'Word of God.' I must have been missing something that would make this all okay. I just needed to find that piece of the puzzle. Perhaps it was within the scriptural text.

In reading along, I began to feel an overwhelming sense of confusion throughout multiple contradicting texts. Here I was trying to get answers so that I could help convert the world, yet I was only becoming more confused. I started to wonder how many people that call themselves 'believers' had actually read the Bible. Surely they had come across these confusing texts as well.

Exodus 15:3 says the Lord is a god of war, but Romans 15:33 says he is a god of peace. Matthew 1:16 says Jacob was Joseph's father, but Luke 3:23 says Joseph was the son of Heli. John 10:30 says that Jesus and Yahweh are one and the same, but in John 14:28, Jesus says, *"the Father is greater than I."* Genesis 7:2 says for Noah to take animals by the 'sevens,' before the great flood, but Genesis 7:9 says for him to take two of each. Matthew 5:1–2 says that Jesus taught his disciples on the top of a mountain, but Luke 6:17–20 says that Jesus came down from the top of the mountain and taught his disciples at the bottom.

What were Jesus' last words? Matthew 27:46–50 says: *"My God My God, why hast thou forsaken me?"* (This is very strange, because he is supposed to be the same as 'God!') But Luke 23:46 says that Jesus' last words were *"Father, unto thy hands I commend my spirit."* However, John 19:30 says that Jesus received the vinegar and said, *"It is finished"* and he bowed his head and "gave up the ghost."

Genesis 32:30 says, *"I have seen God face to face,"* but John 1:18 says that 'God' cannot be seen. Second Kings 2:11 says that Elijah ascended to Heaven *"by a whirlwind."* But John 3:13 says that no man has ascended to Heaven except Jesus. Matthew 5:16 says you should let people see your good deeds. But Matthew 6:3–4 says when you give to the needy, do it in secret, and Yahweh will reward what is done secretly.

The story of the great flood is yet another issue that contemporary thinkers have with the Bible. First of all, Yahweh essentially regrets making humans and animals, when he states in Genesis 6:7, *"I will destroy man whom I have created from the face of the earth; both man and beast, and the creeping thing and the fowls of the air, for it repenteth me that I have made them."* Christian apologists will say that this is not proof of 'God' making a mistake, but instead, the free will of man and the choices humans made caused him to be unhappy with the world he created for us. I'd like to know what the beasts and birds and creeping things did to deserve extermination. Regardless, Yahweh says he is unhappy with the world and wishes to destroy it and all that inhabits it, yet he instructs Noah to save the animals and creeping things. This was strange to me, because if the inhabitants of the earth are what caused it to become viral then saving those same species would just be replanting the same bad seeds of negativity, and that didn't seem to be a very effective form of problem solving for an omniscient being. But after all, I'm only human. What do I know?

I then wanted to challenge if it would even be possible to do what was allegedly accomplished by Noah. According to the World Resources Institute as of 2009, *"scientists have a better understanding of how many stars are in the galaxy, than how many species exists on Earth"* but estimates range from *2—100 million* (WRI 2009). To actually believe that 2 (or 7) of each species including all land animals and insects fit on the same boat, and that Noah could have provided food for all of the animals (somehow keeping the red meat for the carnivores from spoiling), taken care of them, and dealt with the droppings, and stopped them from killing each other for five months, seemed utterly ridiculous to me. Besides, one could only imagine what the termites and woodpeckers would have done to a wooden ark! There are so many fallacies with the story; it was hard for me to keep up or make sense of it.

Former evangelist Charles Templeton writes about the building of the ark, in his book *Farewell to God* (1996),

> *"The impossibility of the undertaking is immediately evident when one realizes that the ark was built in the days before steel. There were no axes, no saws, no hammers, and no nails. Trees had to be felled and fashioned into intersecting and adjoining planks with only the crudest of tools and made watertight with pitch."(55)*

He goes on to have the reader imagine four men and their wives accomplishing this goal in just seven days. But was it really seven days? The scripture does say that 'God' says he will make it rain in seven days, but he says this, some speculate, *after* the ark was already built. That means Noah had seven days to *fill* the ark with animals, not *build* it. Templeton later points out that Noah would have no refrigeration in which to store any fresh meat for the carnivores (56).

Looking now at Exodus 14:22–31 and the story of Moses as he parted the Red Sea, we have a hard time even finding evidence outside the Bible that Moses existed, let alone that there were Jewish slaves in Egypt! Not a single shred of evidence points to Jews in that area at that time, yet the Bible says they were there for forty years. Aside from that, parting an entire sea sounds amazing, when in reality it is possible that a small group of people crossed the *Reed* Sea, during low tides, where a person could actually walk across on a windy day, instead of the Red Sea. If someone were to see this from a distance, there's no doubt they would call it a miracle!

The entire basis of Christianity begins under the assumption that the Bible is the 'Word of God.' Regardless of the many contradictions I listed above, I was positive that if I could prove that the Bible was in fact 'God's Word,' then we could all investigate the meanings of those scriptures at a later time. After all, if the Bible could never be proven to be of holy inspiration, then chasing those rabbits down a hole would be pointless and foolish. So, I set out to discover how a god could write a book for us. Of course, Yahweh didn't actually sit down and write a holy book or instruction manual for us to follow, so how did we get it, and why is it considered 'God's Word?'

As it turns out, the Holy Bible was written over a span of sixteen hundred years in three different languages, by forty different authors, none of whom knew they were writing what would someday be considered one collective book. It was never written as an entire piece of work all at once. Many of the books were 'canonized' as one in the third century.

The Bible was actually formed as a result of the Council of Nicaea in the year 325 CE, at a council headed by Constantine, a Roman Emperor. Consider this from Columbia University:

> When Constantine defeated Emperor Licinius in 323 AD he ended the persecutions against the Christian church. Shortly afterwards Christians faced a trouble from within: the Arian controversy began and threatened to divide the church. The problem began in Alexandria, it started as a debate between the bishop Alexander and the presbyter (pastor, or priest) Arius.

Arius proposed that if the Father begat the Son, the latter must have had a beginning, that there was a time when he was not, and that his substance was from nothing like the rest of creation. The Council of Nicaea, a gathering similar to the one described in Acts 15:4–22, condemned the beliefs of Arius and wrote the first version of the now famous creed proclaiming that the Son was "one in being with the Father" by use of the Greek word "homoousius."

It's evident that the confusion of 'God's Word' is not a new conundrum, and that the Bible was not written by Jehovah himself, so the explanation becomes that it is instead, the *inspired* Word of God,' leaving room for human error. I began to wonder if perhaps some texts that were also inspired did not make it into the canon. Perhaps some things did not agree with Constantine's ruling, so he threw them out. I discovered that there were women who also wrote gospels about Jesus, but those were not allowed in the book, because, well, they were written by women. This started to seem more like the inspired word of *Constantine* than that of any god.

Furthermore, so many people claim to be Christian, yet do not believe in large portions of the Bible, but rather say it is a 'guide' to live by, and that faith takes over when they don't understand. The problem I had with this, is that if they didn't trust the Bible about some things, how would they know they could trust it about others? After all, the only reason many of them know the name Jesus at all, is because of the same book they in turn discredit for some of it's crazy stories. Would 'walking on water,' 'raising the dead,' or perhaps 'being the embodiment of God' not fall into that category?

I didn't understand how someone could claim to have faith in something they didn't fully trust. Isn't that the core meaning of *faith*? To pick and choose from certain portions of the book is both inconsistent, and intellectually dishonest. It is either the word of 'God' or it isn't. And if you've read portions of it, and believe certain things, but ignore others, you may be a *believer*, but you certainly aren't *Christian*.

## ARE YOU CHRISTIAN?

This is probably the most 'loaded' question one could ask. In fact, I think it's safe to say that most people asking it don't even quite understand what they're asking. Aside from answering it, suppose I just asked you to restate the question in different words. More than likely, you would say *"Do you believe in God?"* But are the two questions really equivalent? One thing I discovered on my journey is that one's belief in a god does not constitute Christianity, even if that belief is that Jesus Christ did exist. Which ultimate reality or god does one believe in? If one believes in the god of the Bible and the original Old Testament, do they also follow the teachings of Jesus? In most cases, the answer is no!

Since a Baptist preacher and a Pentecostal churchgoer both proudly called themselves Christians, yet confused me days earlier with their conflicting beliefs, my next move was to define Christianity. How could both of these people have the same religious association, yet disagree with one another? If you ask average Americans if they are Christians, and ask them to state why, you will typically get an answer such as *"Yes, because I believe in God."*

First of all, we have to recognize that most of these people have ignored the fact that *god* is a title, not a name. It's a position of power, or a deity that is said to create matter, or intervene in daily lives through metaphysical powers. There have been thousands of mythical gods in human history. Poseidon, Horus, Demeter, Zeus, and Mithras were also 'gods.' So calling the Christian god simply 'God' is like referring to the person that fixes your car simply as 'Mechanic,' or worse yet, as 'Person.' The god in the Bible is named Yahweh, or Jehovah, but because one is never supposed to speak his name, most Christians rarely recognize this, and simply call him 'God.'

When people say they are 'Christian' what does that really mean? They obviously don't have to agree on all topics (just as Atheists, Democrats, and Muslims disagree on various things with people in their own frame of thinking), because we see that Baptists, Mormons, Catholics, and Pentecostals are all Christians. Most dictionaries simply define *Christian* as one who follows the teachings of Jesus Christ. But what did Jesus Christ teach? What does it mean to follow him?

I've discovered that many people, from living in this society alone, would probably assume that Jesus taught peaceful things and was a great leader who encouraged family values and respect. In fact, if I told you that someone in the Bible arrived on earth and was specifically quoted as saying this, who would you guess it was? *"Do not think that I came to bring peace. I did not come to bring peace, but a sword, for I have come to set a man against his father and a daughter against her mother,"* would you guess it was Satan? It was actually Jesus, in Matthew 10:34–35. When this is brought to the attention of preachers, they turn the focus to the use of the word 'sword' and say it was metaphorical, not literal. That's not the point. Jesus himself said he came to divide families, in fact, some versions of the text use the word 'division' instead of 'sword.' To further the point, verses 36–39 go on to say that anyone who is not willing to turn his back on his family for

Jesus is not worthy of him. I wondered: why would the Bible say such a thing?

It gets a little more confusing if you backtrack and read a few verses above that. Begin at Matthew 10:32, and you will see that Jesus tells us to confess our sins before man, and he will confess before *"My Father in Heaven."* Again, this goes back to my first question of the "father or son" and boggles the mind. If Jesus is the human form of Yahweh, why would he need to confess anything to a third party? Wouldn't he be confessing your sins to himself? This deeply confused me.

So when you say *"Yes, I am Christian, because I believe in God,"* does that really make you Christian? Probably the single most important verses for Christianity are found in the New Testament; more specifically, Matthew 7:21–23, *"Not everyone who says to Me, 'Lord, Lord,' shall enter the kingdom of Heaven, but he who does the will of My father in Heaven. Many will say to Me in that day 'Lord, Lord, have we not prophesied in Your name, cast out demons in Your name, and done many wonders in Your name?' And then I will declare to them, 'I never knew you: depart from Me, you who practice lawlessness!'"*

These verses alone remove most of us from the Christian pool. So what's our next step to getting back into good graces with Jesus? Remember, this was my journey for being a better Christian and discovering the existence of Yahweh. So what piece of information is left? We need to know the *will* of Yahweh, so that we may do that, in order to follow Jesus, enter Heaven, and be a true Christian.

## THE FATHER'S WILL

We often hear *"Let God's will be done."* And Jesus just told us in the New Testament that if we don't do his father's will, we cannot enter Heaven—and that simply believing isn't enough. But what does this god want from us? Jesus is the star of the New Testament, but to learn more about Yahweh and his will, we have to return to the Old Testament, where he was much more involved. We are told that when time comes to an end, we will have to answer for our past. This means that what happened in the past matters to Yahweh. So, I returned to the Bible, where he made it very clear what he wanted from mankind. I had completed Genesis, and although I was a bit taken back and confused by it all, I continued through the Old Testament to find my answers. These are the verses that stood out to me that clearly defined the will of the father.

**Exodus 35:2**, *Work shall be done for six days, but the seventh day shall be a holy for you, a Sabbath of rest to the Lord. Whoever does any work on it shall be put to death.*

**Leviticus 20:10**, *The man who commits adultery with another man's wife, he who commits adultery with his neighbors wife, the adulterer and the adulteress shall surely be put to death.*

**Leviticus 20:13**, *If a man lies with a male as he lies with a woman, both of them have committed an abomination. They shall surely be put to death. Their blood shall be upon them.*

**Leviticus 21:9**, *The daughter of any priest, if she profanes herself by playing the harlot* (becomes a prostitute) *she profanes her father. She shall be burned with fire.*

**Deuteronomy 21:18-21**, *If a man has a stubborn and rebellious son who will not obey the voice of his father or the voice of his mother, and who, when they have chastened him, will not heed them, then his father and his mother shall take hold of him and bring him out to the elders of his city, to the gate of his city, and they shall say to the elders of this city, "This son of ours is stubborn and rebellious, he will not obey our voice, he is a glutton and a drunkard." Then all the men of his city shall stone him to death with stones, so you shall put away the evil from among you and all Israel shall hear and fear.*

One could gather from these texts that if we are not killing homosexuals, killing those who cheat on their spouse, killing misbehaving children, burning prostitutes, and killing those who work on the holy day, we are not doing the will of the *Father* and are therefore not Christians at all and will be denied by Jesus in the end. Granted, the New Testament Christians are about to throw this book across the room in frustration, because I haven't mentioned that the coming of Christ and the New Testament cancels out all those rules, so we aren't supposed to do those things anymore. Again, at this point you must decide whether you will accept that answer in faith and move on, or investigate. I chose the latter.

The investigator cannot turn away from the fact that Yahweh ordered death and destruction of so many people in the Old Testament and did not stop the massacres until he witnessed the torture and death of himself in human form; and only then, did he feel as though 'we were even.' And if the New Testament brings about a change which repeals the Old Testament (as my New Testament Christian readers would say), then why do we still worry with the Ten Commandments or Old Testament at all?

Moreover, if *our* past matters, Yahweh's past matters; so I ask you again; are you Christian? Do you in fact do the will of the father, and do you even understand what that means? If I was wrong in my assertion of this, I would've loved to be enlightened. This was a rough one for me, and I still did not fully understand what the will of the father was, or what I should do to enter the Kingdom with Jesus according to his instructions in the book of Matthew.

Often times, we tend to only examine ourselves and our circumstances from the angle in which we see it, and I feel like that is a big part of our failure to grow as a society. If our perception is our reality, sometimes we need to change our perception, to check the validity of our reality. This is why I stepped outside the box of Christianity for my investigation, to see how other people view the Christian church. I looked at the strongest and most popular opponent of Christians, the Atheists, to see what they thought about Christianity and how it was perceived.

Dr. David Eller explains very clearly in his book *Atheism Advanced* (2007) that Christianity is not *a* religion at all, but a collection of religions and systems of beliefs. One of the most compelling arguments I've ever heard in the case of Atheism is by Dr. Eller, when he compares religions to languages, as all have their own 'scripts' and 'rituals'—just as you would say *"how are you?"* and my natural response is *"fine"* regardless of how my day is *actually* going. He makes the point that we have habits and languages ingrained in our brains and we utilize these scripts daily. One could never say that English is *truer* than Spanish, because they are different languages. This is also why Catholicism is no *truer* than Mormonism. They are all basically sets of scripts and rituals that have their own purpose but do not represent factual truth. Dr. Eller also warns of non-believers and those of other religions doing what he calls *"speaking-Christian."* Often times, we take words like *Heaven, Hell, angels, demons,* and *sin,* and consider them to be absolutes, when in fact thousands of religions across the world do not recognize such metaphysical things (33–66). The young boy living in a jungle near Zimbabwe may practice religious rituals in *animism* or *ancestor worship,* but he has no fear of *demons* or *Hell,* nor does he even have a concept to relate these things. They simply do not exist to him because he has never been taught about them. In his world, most 'ghosts' are good things—spirits that watch over his family and property.

In light of this viewpoint from the Atheists, it was interesting to see a different perception of Christianity. They weren't as 'opposed' to my original beliefs as I had once thought. Instead, I had discovered that they were basically 'discrediting' those beliefs along with all other religions that made claims that couldn't be proven outside of faith. Atheism was not in *opposition* to religious beliefs, but rather *aside* from them all.

I found this to be very interesting but had no intention of joining these Atheists in their thought process. After all, I felt bad enough by not being a good Christian and having doubts. The last thing I wanted to do was denounce 'God' altogether! I needed to know what I could do to have even stronger faith—and so the search continued.

# CHAPTER 2: PASSING JUDGMENT

## POPULAR LABELS

The shocking new definitions of 'Christian' gathered from reading the Bible confirmed my skepticism, but fired up my search for the truth. For some reason, I felt the need to put a label on myself and others. Could I still consider myself a Christian with the amount of doubts I had? In public I certainly could! Surely, I just needed more information. I couldn't defect from the Christian faith simply based on a few verses in the Bible—or could I? I thought to myself, "Perhaps there is a denomination within Christianity that has the same problems with the doctrine that I do." In fact, I needed to know what other religions believed that claimed to have the truth. I only knew of Muslims, Mormons, Jews, and Atheists from what my preacher had mentioned in church. I had never really looked into those labels myself. I wondered, "What do Muslims and Jews believe differently from Christians? What are Mormons really all about? What is an Atheist?" These are the questions I posed for myself as my journey continued.

If I don't know what separates myself from these labels, how am I sure that I don't agree with their views? I didn't want to be the common American stubborn mule with the stance of "Jesus is real, so don't question it." Besides, that wouldn't be 'knowing in my heart,' so it wouldn't really count. I knew that there were large numbers of very intelligent people who had other beliefs (and non-beliefs), and I wanted to know why and what really separated them from me. Essentially, I was making a list, and crossing each of them off to end up with Christianity as the best possible choice.

As part of my research, I consulted with a person dedicated to each of the following groups, and with their approval, compiled a quick description of the most common categories related to religion we hear about in the United States. Hopefully, this will clear up common misconceptions for you as it did for me.

**MUSLIM:** One who believes the religious faith of Islam, known as a *monotheistic* religion (worshiping just one god, like Christianity) including belief in *Allah* as the sole god and in Muhammad as his prophet. Muslims read the Holy Qur'an (Koran) instead of the Bible. This is very much like the Christian faith with a major fundamental difference. Jesus is given great honor in the Qur'an as a prophet and miracle-worker, but he is not said to be a god, nor the son of any god. Also, it is unthinkable to the teachings of Islam that a prophet of a god could die a horrible shameful death like a crucifixion. So the Qur'an claims that Jesus didn't die on the cross, Judas died in his place because Allah made him look like Jesus as payback for his wicked betrayal. Muslims by nature are not violent people. The attacks you hear about on the news are from Muslim extremists, who do not represent the majority of the religious population, yet they do have religious doctrine to back up their violent acts.

**MORMON:** 'Mormon' is really just a nickname for those who belong to the 'LDS' or *Church of Jesus Christ of Latter Day Saints* and believe in the *Book of Mormon* as "another testament of Jesus Christ," which Joseph Smith wrote after saying he translated ancient writings. There was a rocky beginning to the religion, since

Smith did not speak or read the language of those original writings. The group as a whole believes in Jesus Christ, and the Father, Yahweh (or Elohim) as the Lord. Mormons are Christians because they do follow the teachings of Jesus. However, they also believe that Jesus and Elohim are in flesh and bone in Heaven and that Joseph Smith was a prophet who had visions in which Elohim spoke to him. Modern day prophets are also said to exist in the Mormon Church, with Elohim speaking directly to the highest member, the current prophet, who has twelve apostles. Mormons are often associated with polygamy (multiple wives) because of old doctrines within the church, but the majority of them have since abandoned that notion in light of modern laws which prohibit such marriages. However, they do believe that upon dying, when a man enters the Celestial Kingdom, he openly practices polygamy, as ordained by 'God.' Some fundamentalist Mormons still hold true to the polygamist way of life in the natural world, and go by 'FLDS,' with men marrying multiple women, and often, very young ones. The 'Holy Capital' of the LDS Church is Salt Lake City, Utah.

**JEW:** The Jewish people only consider the 'Old Testament' of the Bible to be true and in fact study this collection as a different book, called the Tanakh. Jews do not support the Bible as a whole. They believe Jesus Christ lived, and was a teacher, but was not the Messiah, nor the son of Yahweh. Therefore, Jews are theists, but not Christians. They have suffered a tremendous history of persecution, mostly due to the stigma of being responsible for the crucifixion of Jesus Christ. This issue is debatable, and the Bible even points to doubt in the New Testament, in the Book of

John 19:12 as it states: *Everyone who makes himself a king sets himself against Caesar.* This statement suggests that Jesus could have been killed for defying the Roman Empire and considering himself a king, as a threat to Caesar. However, others point to the Jews setting Jesus up because he claimed to be the son of Yahweh, which they worshipped. It is quite difficult to become Jewish if you decide to convert and can take up to two years to complete the intense process. Jews do not celebrate Christmas.

**CHRISTIAN:** One who professes belief in the teachings of Jesus Christ and believes he was the human form of Yahweh, and a part of the Holy Trinity (Father, Son, and Holy Ghost). This is not a religion, but rather a collection of religions which have split and evolved over time. The basis of Christianity includes a belief in the teachings of Jesus Christ (hence the word *Christian*), but the term Christian embraces Catholic, Protestant, Methodist, Baptist, Mormon, Lutheran, Anglican, Presbyterian, and others that have been created and split over time. To be clear, one who does not profess a specific belief in any one denomination or set of beliefs in Christianity is simply a theist, not a Christian.

**THEIST:** One who believes in a god or gods as the creator and ruler of the universe. All Christians, Muslims, and Jews are theists (because they worship a god) but some theists do not identify themselves with a religion at all, yet believe a particular god regulates our world with laws and responds to prayers. Theism is a very broad belief: simply professing a higher power exists and controls the world. So Christians are theists, but not all theists are Christian.

**DEIST:** One who believes in a system of thought advocating natural religion, emphasizing morality, and denying the interference of a creator with the laws of the universe. Deists believe a *deity* (a god) exists, and perhaps created the universe, but does not regulate the life therein with laws of religion, commandments, or prayer answering. This is sometimes noted as being a hybrid belief of evolution and creationism, meaning that the deity created conditions for life, yet allowed evolution to run its course without interference. This was the majority belief system of the Founding Fathers of the United States. Few were actually Christians, although some of them spoke of 'God' as the deity in common language.

**ATHEIST:** The word 'Atheist' had always left a bad taste in my mouth. It was practically a synonym for 'evil' or 'bad' as I was growing up, and I never really understood why. Most of the people in the Bible Belt will tell you they actually believe that Atheists *"worship the Devil."* There is such a misunderstanding associated with the word that President George H.W. Bush actually said, *"I don't know that Atheists should be considered as citizens"* (1996).

So what is an Atheist? To find out, we must review a quick origin of words. 'Theos' is the Greek word for *god.* 'Atheos' is Greek for *'without gods.'* This is the same root word that spawned 'theist' above, 'theology' (the study of gods), and 'theologian' (a specialist in religion or gods). Moreover, a 'polytheist' is one who believes in multiple gods (such as the Greeks). We've all heard of Greek mythology, where they basically assigned a different god to specific parts of nature. When Christians were first introduced, they were referred to as 'Atheos' because the Christians denied the multiple gods and claimed that Jesus was the one true god. Christians were thereby 'atheistic' toward the gods of that time. In fact, as you read this today, you probably don't believe in the Greek gods or any of the Hindu or Norse gods. Therefore, as a Christian or theist, you are *atheistic* to all gods other than the Christian one. An Atheist simply believes in one less god than that, and they feel that the metaphysical claims made by Christians are just as impractical as the ones made by Satanists, Greeks, or Hindus. Atheists do not believe in blind faith, ghosts, spirits, gods, angels, demons, devils, or anything else in the spiritual world, but prefer to live by means of Secular Humanism. Atheists are simply without any god at all.

**SECULAR HUMANISM:** A lifestyle that promotes human values without specific reference to religious doctrines. All Atheists, Agnostics, and Deists, by necessity, are also Secular Humanists.

**EVOLUTIONIST:** One who understands the scientific evidence that describes evolution, which explains that the various types of animals and plants have their origin in other preexisting types and that the distinguishable differences are due to modifications in successive generations. Charles Darwin's *Theory of Evolution by Means of Natural Selection* simply states that all living things have a common ancestor. He does not assert that humans popped out of monkeys, or that a "blob can become your friend" as many Christian apologists like to make you believe. The theory does teach, however, that monkeys and humans are related to common ancestors as fossil records indicate, as are all things through time and adaptation. Regardless of your take on this, the fact remains that humans share about 98.9% of genetic DNA with chimpanzees.

**AGNOSTIC:** This one is difficult to define. Typically, an agnostic is described as one who believes it is impossible to know whether any god exists; but when you really think of it, that describes all of us. The fact remains that it is impossible to have all knowledge of the universe. It really just comes down to what you consider as proof or reliable methods of obtaining knowledge. I've read multiple definitions of agnosticism, and many are conflicting, but here's my take on it: deciding whether you're Atheist or Agnostic is really pointless. You either have faith or you don't. An Agnostic is not *skeptical* of unicorns or leprechauns; they are not 'undecided' about the Tooth Fairy. So why claim to be skeptical of a religion? If one claims to be Agnostic, what is the name of their god? If they do not have one, then they are an Atheist—without gods, yet they claim to be Agnostic as some sort of insurance policy as if 'undecided' is any better than Atheistic.

**BIG BANG THEORY:** A theory which describes the expansion of the universe from a singularity, then to our universe as we know it. No massive collision of rocks or stars created the Big Bang, nor was it actually a 'bang' at all. According to the standard theory, our universe began to expand from a 'singularity' around 13.7 billion years ago. Galaxies currently appear to be moving away from us at speeds proportional to their distance (Hubble, 1929). This observation supports the expansion of the universe and suggests that it was once compacted and began expanding as it is today. There are still many questions about the theory, and probably the strongest argument used by theistic apologists during debates is *"what created the big bang?"* We do not yet know.

**CREATIONIST:** One who believes in the creation of the world and universe by a higher power and is opposed to the Big Bang Theory and Darwin's *Theory of Evolution by Means of Natural Selection.* One such notion of creationism is stated in the Bible, Genesis 1:1–3 *In the beginning God created the Heavens and the earth. And the earth was without form, and void; and darkness was upon the face of the deep. And the Spirit of God moved upon the face of the waters. And God said, Let there be light: and there was light.*

Many words in the English language may be misunderstood, simply due to years of slanted world views. For example, you would be instantly offended if someone called you an 'infidel' or 'heathen.' These terms have long been regarded by the general public as insults and claims of someone being a lower class citizen, a nuisance, or a threat to society. I took a moment to think about what each of these words meant to me, and then researched the definitions for a clearer view.

**HEATHEN:** An unconverted individual of a people who do not acknowledge the god of the Bible; a person who is neither a Jew, Christian, nor Muslim. This term has long been regarded as a 'bad person' or used to refer to a child as *out of control*, or a brat, when in reality, it's just an Atheist or a person belonging to a religion other than the ones listed above. So, Hindus are heathens, and if you are simply theistic, without a specific tie to a Christian denomination, you are a heathen as well, which basically makes this a useless term, as it explains most of us in one way or another.

**INFIDEL:** One who doubts or rejects a particular doctrine, system, or principle, including religious documents or concepts. So, any person who has ever questioned the Bible has been an infidel, but if you believe in the Bible and question the Qur'an as valid, you are also an infidel, because the Qur'an contains a religious doctrine. Our society has made asking questions worthy of an insult! In fact, 'infidelity' means both *cheating on your spouse*, and *doubting religion*. Why would the two be associated? The answer is simple. It comes down to a lack of trust. You either do not trust your god, or you're not worthy of trust from your spouse. It causes your peers to doubt you, and you become an outsider. Challenging questions are often frowned upon because they are an attempt to obtain knowledge. Knowledge is power, and many extreme religious leaders want us to remain powerless, needing them for guidance and acceptance. Therefore, you will be ashamed to ask questions for fear of being an *infidel* and regarded as a lower class or threat.

Alright, now I was really afraid. I had officially questioned the religious doctrine of Christianity. Did that make me an infidel? I couldn't accept that. I was just a young Christian with questions, and there shouldn't be anything wrong with that! But why was I so afraid?

Many religions encourage you to follow the masses blindly under the concept of faith, where questions are not permitted and fearful worship is commanded. Napoleon Bonaparte once said *"Religion is excellent stuff for keeping common people quiet."* This is made true by changing the common vocabulary (as I've previously outlined) to create a negative association with words that are not part of the religious beliefs. But certainly this was not Christianity, for I had been invited to ask questions, and sit with preachers to find my answers. But I quickly discovered as each of their explanations received a rebuttal from me as I tried to make sense of it all, that we no longer had the understanding that we are all just different. Instead, the sociological mind-set became: if you're not with us, you're against us, and are therefore bad—and the new enemy. This statement comes almost word for word from the New Testament writings of both Matthew and Mark.

This creates the situation Napoleon was referring to, and the common people stayed together for fear of being ostracized or attacked for disagreeing with the masses. As an example, in my teenage years, I wasn't even aware of what an Atheist actually was. I was afraid to even utter the term because it sounded so evil to me. I had always been taught that people who were heathens or Atheists were a clear abomination of Jesus Christ and would perish in Hell. For some reason, I also had the understanding that

Atheists were somehow connected with devil-worship. You may feel the same, and that's normal because of the society in which most of us were raised.

It's so ingrained in our heads from such a young age that even when we discover facts against our beliefs, we shun them out of habit or perhaps fears of actually seeing a valid argument against our faith. With this in mind, being that fear and 'God' have been ingrained in you since an early age, you just can't bring yourself to even utter phrases such as *"There is no god."* If you were to try it, you would get an uncomfortable feeling because it just doesn't sound right, even if you don't mean it. If you were just brave enough to do it, you know what I mean!

But is this a result of 'God' being within us all? Or is it instead a process of 'psychological modeling' in an influential religious environment that has shaped us to feel this way? The problem is, something that is metaphysical looks the same as if it weren't real at all, so it's very hard to tell the difference between what we hope is there, and what is actually making a difference in our lives. That fear of being wrong is what should motivate research and understanding, not prevent it. That's ultimately what did it for me, and why I began this research.

# FREE WILL: DO WE REALLY HAVE A CHOICE?

My next question along the journey was, *"Why do we have the ability to choose against God?"* One would think that if the Christian god exists, he would make it impossible for us to fail and have everyone follow him back home to the paradise of a Heavenly afterlife. When I presented this question to my preacher, he responded by saying, *"God doesn't force you to choose him so that you will have free will."* It appeared to be an excellent point to me, but I did wonder why a perfect god would create a being bound to fail, and how we could be considered 'free' if we are going to be punished for making the wrong decisions. After all, I'm not free to speed on the highway or shoot random people—I am punished for those actions.

The preacher continued by asking me if I would want one of my children to be forced into loving me, or if I would want them to choose me. Of course, we'd all want our children to choose us, so he felt his case was made pretty easily. But our children's love cannot be coerced, it must be earned. There are several adults I know that have a parent they've never seen or heard from, and do not love at all. If we mistreat our children, or otherwise act inconsistently toward them, including not making ourselves apparent in their lives, we could not rightly expect their love. My answer to his question made the conversation uncomfortable. *"Of course I would want my child to choose me, but I could never, under any circumstances, force my child to undergo torture and fire for denying me, or anything else for that matter."* Moreover, that only evolved my question into: *"Do we really have free will in the first place, or do we choose under duress?"*

It's quite difficult, when discussing free will, not to enter the realm of philosophy. What is *free*? What is *will*? What is a *choice*? To save you the headache many of my college professors have given me, I won't go into the details of ancient perceptions of life and matter. I will say, however, that it's not even an important deciding factor of Christianity's truthfulness to determine whether or not we have free will. If one of the *determinist* nature presents evidence that we don't have free will, the believer will say that our will must match "God's will" for it to be done. If one asserts that the Christian god wasn't there for him or her in a time of need, then the response from the believer is that "God allows you to make your own choices and accept your own consequences." It doesn't seem to matter which direction we go with this question, the doubter is trapped either way. Or is it the believer that's trapped? One may wish to claim that the notion of free will is proof that Christianity is true. But is it? Must we disprove reincarnation to refute Hinduism?

When you break it down, isn't free will just about a choice? If you have any choice at all, regardless of the consequences, then that constitutes free will, right? Let me challenge you for a moment, as I challenged myself. Consider this: if I hand you my keys and say, *"You can choose to drive my car away right now; it's totally up to you,"* that is your choice. But as you grab my keys and start towards my car, I also say, *"But if you do take my car, you must know that I will push this button which detonates a bomb in the car, killing everyone within 100 feet of the blast, including you; but you still have total free will to take my car."* Is that really free will? I suppose technically, you have the choice to make, but at some point we have to recognize duress and consequence as pertinent factors of the decision making process and openly admit they play a mighty role.

We'd like to think (in the Christian world view) that we have a choice in the matter. But when faced with consequences of eternal damnation and the fiery depths of Hell, the coercion reaches new heights. It's no longer really about a choice. It's about what you're willing to chance for your freedom on earth and the gamble you're taking that the Christian god is actually a reasonable guy that will give *you* an exception.

Isn't that really what Christians mean when they claim to have a "personal relationship with God," as if they have a VIP pass or a back-door entrance into Heaven? Of course this also means that the personal relationship status exempts them from being subject to judgment for activities such as smoking, drinking, cursing, fighting, divorce, fornication, homosexuality, adultery, greed, and not attending church. They have a personal relationship with their god, so those little things don't matter; yet the Bible strictly speaks against these actions and repeatedly says there are no exceptions. The ironic part of it is, these same people will look to an agnostic or Atheist and tell them how they are going to Hell for not "living right by God." These are the misled individuals who are in turn misleading their children and misleading society about their own religious beliefs and practices. They are the epitome of the hypocrite. I wanted to understand them too, for perhaps I was one of them.

## HEAVEN & HELL

I often wondered why religion was even a topic at all. The reason is a hopeful eternal existence, of course. Isn't it? Or is that why *Christianity* is a topic? Perhaps religion itself is about something more. I began to see religion in a different light, and no longer equated it with Christianity, for the two are not the same. After all, at some point in life, everyone wants to know where they will end up for eternity, or what the meaning of life really is, if there is one at all. But not only Christians wonder this. There are tales of spirituality and metaphysical beings in every culture, even those without Christianity, angels, demons, gods, and spirits. I wondered where we got this notion of Heaven and Hell, and if all religions had similar places of glory and punishment.

Many Christians will candidly admit to sporadically attending church to prevent a visit to Hell (as if a few Sundays a year when it's convenient, or on holidays, are a logical trade off for eternal happiness with Jesus). But do we ever stop to think about where Hell is, and what could happen in such a place? Do we ever stop to consider other potential reasons for these stories?

There are many possible origins of the concept of Hell, but my focus was not on the historicity—but on the possibility. More than likely, Hell was said to be *underground* because of the volcanic activity, cracks in the rock, and fiery explosions that happened from below. The myths that could originate from archaic men witnessing such powerful nature are countless, and would no doubt include a fiery underworld.

In my quest for finding the truth, I had to ponder a few points that are commonly overlooked when discussing eternal pain and punishment. In most Christian beliefs, (excluding the Mormons) when people die, their bodies are left here, while their souls move on to a *spirit* world of either Heaven or Hell (or perhaps purgatory if you're Catholic).

First of all, fire and heat are both physical properties, not spiritual. That's like saying you're taking your Chevy with you to Heaven! How could a physical attribute be present in a non-physical environment? It just doesn't make logical sense. Secondly, if our bodies are left here, what would we *feel* things with? Our nerve endings are all located in the physical body we've left behind. So effectively, if there were some sort of after-life pain or fire to be felt, we wouldn't feel it!

Even after debunking the myth of an actual existence of a place dedicated to eternal pain and suffering, I had to wonder exactly why such a place would be created at all. Perhaps just *not entering Heaven* would have been a sufficient punishment and would still suffice free will; but was eternal pain and suffering really necessary? Although the Bible tells us that only the Heavens and the earth were created in the beginning, one would have to think that it would fall under all of creation, which means the god of the Bible would have had to construct the punishment chamber as well.

In traveling along this particular philosophical portion of my journey, I completed the following exercise, and I will ask you to do the same. Stop and think for a moment, about when you've witnessed suffering of any type. Begin with memories of a pet dog or cat and watching it deal with a thorn, and how it hopped along as its paw remained elevated and curved as it whimpered or cried. Now, what if your beloved pet had attacked someone the night before? Would you still pull the thorn out, or would you leave it in for punishment? If not, how long would you watch the animal suffer? A week? A month? Eternity?

This next one is difficult to write, so I'm sure it will be difficult to read, but we must take it to the next level to get just a glimpse of how this all works. Now, imagine for a moment that the thorn is in the foot of your small daughter. This is a little girl that you created, and she's screaming in agony, crying for you to help, and you are standing there watching the tears roll down her face as she lies helpless in the dirt. Then you realize, she has fallen into an ant bed, and fire ants begin to cover her body. Her screams are heartbreaking as the ants enter her mouth and become relentless. She feels so helpless, and you're the only one that can stop her pain. She reaches out for you and screams for help. You look into her eyes and calmly say, *"I'm sorry; but yesterday you said that you didn't believe I was your parent, so now I do not know you."* Could you watch? Would you turn and walk away, hearing her screams in the distance?

This is exactly what the Bible says Jesus will do if you simply do not believe in him. If you doubt his existence, or if you don't have faith, he will turn away from you as you suffer and scream for help. He will say *"I do not know you."* That will make one either become terrified and worship out of fear, or make one angry at the possibility of being left behind over a technicality, when so many facts are left unanswered, and so many details are confusing or contradictory. The nastiest people I know couldn't walk away from that little girl, let alone *their own* little girl screaming in agony. How could something that was loving and peaceful do it without blinking an eye? If you were a witness to such a situation, and saw a powerful being turn his back on someone so helpless in so much pain, I don't think you could call that being 'holy,' 'peaceful,' or even 'God,' regardless of what that person had done in the past.

In looking at eternal punishment, we can see that the existence of Hell and the concept of eternal punishment are equally as confusing as eternal salvation. After all, where is Heaven? Genesis 1:7–8 begins: *And God said, 'Let there be a firmament in the midst of the waters, and let it divide the waters from the waters.' And God made the firmament, and divided the waters which were under the firmament from the waters which were above the firmament: and it was so. And God called the firmament Heaven.*

According to scripture, Heaven is in the sky, as an arch above the water (and apparently *below* water as well!). In fact, Jesus was said to have 'ascended' into Heaven after his resurrection. This belief created two problems for me. For one, we're back to the *physical body* vs. *spiritual place* issue, and for another, 'ascension' means to *travel up,* so where *exactly* did he go? We know now, after traveling in airplanes, and even into space, that there is no 'firmament' in the sky. It appears dome-shaped because of the shape of our planet, which is a sphere, that we can only see one half of. We also know that no physical body could withstand passing through the earth's atmosphere without disintegrating. But even if Jesus did get through the atmosphere, there is nothing but black space above that, and there is certainly no 'arch,' nor would that be considered 'sky' any longer, but dark space.

Heaven would have to exist below space, but above the waters. More than likely, we travel through what the uneducated men of biblical times called 'Heaven' each time we're on an airplane. They never imagined being able to travel at 37,000 feet! But now that we do, we know better.

When I posed this question to preachers and apologists along the way, they said that Heaven was in a spiritual place, not physically visible in the human world we know. But if that were true, why would the Bible be so direct in giving a physical location just above earth? This was yet another inconsistency I couldn't wrap my head around.

## WHY DO WE PRAY?

We are often caught up in school prayer, public prayer, prayers at dinner, and prayers in hospitals next to sick patients, and we typically fall right in line with it; but have we ever actually thought about why? I did, and I really couldn't get a straight answer out of anyone. During long prayers, or public prayers in churches we often hear the prayer leader say things like *"Lord, let your blessing be upon those attending tonight, and keep us safe as we travel home."* A common thing to say when you hear someone is sick, is *"Our thoughts and prayers are with the family."* However, these same people will tell you that the Christian god is all powerful, all knowing, and everywhere and what he wants to happen will happen. Are we supposed to follow the logic that we are worthless little sinners, and Yahweh is an all powerful god, yet we can direct him on what to do with the balance of the universe with a private mention in prayer? It's a bit strange to say the least. Abortion is viewed as interfering with 'God's will,' but praying for a dying person to live is not? I just couldn't follow the logic no matter how hard I tried, so I looked into this further.

We are supposed to believe that an amazingly powerful being created the universe but needs our direction to either help Nancy in the hospital bed, or to *decide* to help her nonetheless. He allegedly created man from dust but has to be reminded to keep us safe on our drive home. I figured this to be a ridiculous notion. If it is Yahweh's will for a family member to die, who are we to stop it, but mere beggars? If twenty of us ask, will he change his mind? Or has his mind already been made up, because he is outside of time itself, and has therefore already witnessed the death, and knows when it will happen?

I was beginning to realize that Christians place holy and mystical attributes on 'God' when they are making the case for why we should join them in worship, but they will also place human limitations on that same god when it's convenient to prove a point or explain a fallacy in the doctrine. This just wasn't good enough for me. Stepping back and seeing prayer for what it was, I finally decided my view on it: just as funerals are for the dead, and not the living, religions are for the people, not the gods. The same holds true for prayer. It's really just about saying these things aloud and transferring the burden from your shoulders to a metaphysical leader in an effort to remove your own responsibility in the matter. After all, I suppose it works for those who believe it. The burden seems to leave them. But few things frustrate me more than the phrase *"Let go, and let God."*

Regardless of which god you worship, we are each responsible for our own destiny, and those that place their lives and hardships in the hands of another, including any god, are those that have given up on themselves. This viewpoint was not so popular in the circles of reasoning among my Christian brethren. I noticed the circle began to break, and I was no longer being seen as a Christian that was asking questions but rather a heretic out to destroy the Christian faith. That wasn't it at all, I was objectively searching for the answers, and the ones I was finding were not making sense to me. However, I was accused of "choosing against God," and I couldn't figure out why.

# CHAPTER 3: INSTINCTIVE SINS

## ABSOLUTE MORALITY

Furthering my knowledge of Christianity, I of course sat down with a professor of theology from a local university. I didn't get to speak very much before he could tell where I stood in my search for the objective truth. He calmly said, *"Do you believe in absolute morality?"* What followed was probably the longest pause I'd ever taken in a conversation. I knew it was a loaded question, but I wanted to be honest with him, and most importantly, myself. I began thinking out loud, *"An absolute moral would be one that has a final good outcome, and could never be the wrong decision."* He just smiled at me. I said *"My answer is no."* He seemed to be a little taken back by my answer, as he said *"No one ever says 'no' to that. They list rape, murder, and crimes against children, and quickly say 'of course there are morals that are absolute;' you must tell me why you answered no."*

My response was quick and to the point. *"For there to be absolute morality, we would first need to have an absolute source from which that morality derived. Without that source being proven as absolute, we cannot say that any rule is for certain."* I was nineteen years old, and had just confused this man who had taught theology nearly as long as I'd been walking. We sat in silence, both amazed at what had just taken place. He had no rebuttal. He knew the Christian system was built on faith, not empirical evidence. I was actually coming to him for guidance back toward 'God,' and his only response was *"Well, perhaps I should change what I've been teaching my students, and challenge them to think*

Baptized Atheist

*a little harder about that. You're right; there is no absolute source, except for our belief, and beliefs aren't absolute."*

Allow me to pause for a moment and take a brief break from the story of my journey, and challenge the reader directly. You must ponder for yourself: do you believe in absolute knowledge or morals? Are there absolute wrongs? If so, do you believe in these because of your religion or a holy book? This question is vital to your daily decision making, and how you treat others around you, so please think about this carefully.

*Absolute* is typically defined as follows: (1) Something that is free from any restriction or condition. (2) Something that is perfect or complete. This question is directly asking you if you think there are any absolute wrong decisions. Is rape always wrong? Is murder? Are there any morals that are absolute? As a group, most Christians say yes. Now, let's discuss reality.

Before I turned my academic focus to psychology, I studied criminal law. During that time, I discovered that our judicial system has a term called *justifiable homicide* in which a murder is considered legal. This is the rare occurrence of a defender killing an attacker, or any other event where murder was necessary to defeat a threat. So even our government realizes sometimes things aren't what they appear, and there are actually occasions where a murder is the best decision. This removes *murder* from the absolute-wrong category because there are situations that make it the best decision, which causes the least amount of harm to innocence.

From the Christian perspective, the Bible doesn't go into such specifics. It simply says "Thou Shalt Not Kill." Is it really that cut and dried? No one should kill, or it's a sin? If so, and every murderer is going to Hell, ask the next preacher you see why it states in Genesis 22:1–19, that Yahweh ordered Abraham to murder his only son Isaac as a "holocaust" or sacrifice to prove his love. Ask him why Yahweh requested Israel to kill its enemy warriors. What's ethically right about commanding those murders? Where is the *absolute* morality? If there was a reason such war or sacrifice was commanded, then in the eyes of the god of that era, it was justified, and therefore, not immoral. Should Abraham be sent to Hell for attempting to carry out a murder commanded by his god? If our thoughts being impure can also damn us to punishment, and "Thou shalt not kill" is an absolute law, then yes—otherwise, murder is not *absolutely* wrong.

It's hard to argue on the side of absolute morality or knowledge. The reason is (as I told the theology professor) that Christians can hardly claim a copyright on absolute morals, due to the lack of evidence of their source. Meanwhile, nonreligious people have evidence of ethical living in society, which proves that religion is not necessary for morals to exist. It has been made obvious that religious people can act immorally. One only needs to peer into the history of Catholic priests, or preachers turned con-men to prove this fact. And although most religions contain ethical systems, it is not true that all ethical systems are religiously based; therefore, there is no absolute connection between any particular religion and morality (Thiroux & Krasemann, 2009 p. 21).

It seems like a quick and easy answer to state that Christians have the Ten Commandments to guide morality; but which commandment tells us that it's wrong for a twenty-five year old female to have sexual relations with a sixteen year old male? After all, according to United States law, that's pedophilia, but it doesn't violate one of the commandments. So in the Christian view, is it really wrong? Moreover, which commandment suggests that it's wrong for a Christian to take the parking spot of another Christian? In our society, it's ethically wrong to cut someone off and jump ahead of them, but there is no commandment that states "Thou Shalt Wait Thy Turn!" It's impossible to take ten simple statements (only six of which apply to ethical behavior toward one another) and try to make them fit into a life filled with decisions that affect other people.

Think for a moment about how illusions work. You are presented with a visual appearance that leads you to perceive and expect a specific outcome, yet somehow, some way, the unexpected happens. That's only because you don't have all the facts. If you knew what was going on you wouldn't be surprised at all. Metaphorically speaking, you are basically walking through life viewing one big illusion, understanding only a small percentage of what you see, and only making decisions from one perspective. Stop and think sometimes that if you don't agree with something, it doesn't make it 'wrong' or 'stupid.' There just may be circumstances you don't quite understand or are unaware of. Having this approach in life will help you become much more open-minded and generally caring about the situations and circumstances which cause people to do certain things.

The goal here is, when you are presented with facts; don't just jump to judgment of someone else because you don't agree with the outcome, assuming they need to have your same idea of 'God' or that they must be tainted by evil spirits. Think for a moment that there may be circumstances that caused a person to make that decision. Give them the benefit of the doubt for having knowledge or a perception that may be invisible to you.

Furthermore, don't get your ethics from a book, regardless of how holy you think it is. Books are written by humans, including this one, and are subject to error and human fallibility. Obtain your ethics and self respect from your personal experiences and base them on accepted sociological norms, how you want to live, and how you want to be treated, and most importantly, make decisions based on what causes the least amount of harm. There is no black and white, wrong or right. Just be you and treat every human you meet with the utmost respect.

Closing my point from the discussion with the professor, we talked for several hours into the night. Ultimately, I realized that we get our ethics from dealing with one another and our own personal experiences. The Bible may mention our morals, but it was not by any means an absolute source, and should not be considered as such.

# GIFTS TO YAHWEH

In looking at the amazing morals we are allegedly given by the Christian god, and looking over what that god's will is, in an effort to determine what will make him happy, I simply couldn't ignore the order of gifts to be brought to him. What I discovered was shocking. I'm not talking about roses and wine, here!

When you think of human sacrifice, or animal sacrifice, what do you think of? More than likely, you associate those events with satanic rituals. We have always associated the concept of sacrificing life with evil or sadistic practices. How crazy would it be to imagine millions of people across the modern world, including U.S. citizens, worshiping a god that demanded sacrificial animals and humans? Does it sound satanic to you? Well, it's not. It's Christianity.

As I briefly mentioned earlier, Genesis 22: 1–19 begins with the *Testing of Abraham* in which Yahweh tells Abraham directly to kill his son Isaac as a human sacrifice and as proof that he loves Yahweh. (My first thought upon reading this was, *"If Yahweh already knew everything, he would know that Abraham loves him, and there would be no need for a test in the first place!"*). But the order was made nonetheless. The actual command of the child's death is in verse 2. *"Then God said, take your son, your only son, Isaac, whom you love, and go to the region of Moriah. Sacrifice him there as a burnt offering."*

Upon reading this verse, I was astonished that Christians knowingly worship and pray to this god, calling him 'loving' and 'caring' and defending his 'righteousness.' My thoughts were, perhaps they didn't know about this or simply didn't understand it. I was amazed that so many people could proudly follow a god who has commanded such an evil atonement.

It gets even more chilling as the two are walking to the mountain where the child's murder is set to take place under Yahweh's orders. Verse 6 continues: *As the two of them went on together, Isaac spoke up and said to his father Abraham, "Father?" "Yes, my son?" Abraham replied. "The fire and wood are here," Isaac said, "but where is the lamb for the burnt offering?" Abraham answered, "God himself will provide the lamb for the burnt offering, my son." And the two of them went on together.*

This child was following his father with trust and love, never knowing the entire time that he planned to tie him down and murder him as a sacrifice to his god. It is spine tingling, how callused Abraham could be, focused on murdering his son. The text continues by stating that Abraham then ties his son down and is about to stab him to death when a voice from Heaven suddenly stops him and says, *"Do not lay a hand on the boy. Now I know that you fear me, because you have not withheld from me your son, your only son."* Even with this stoppage of murder, an animal sacrifice is still necessary to satisfy this god's ego. The text continues: *Abraham looked up and there in a thicket he saw a ram caught by its horns. He went over and took the ram and sacrificed it as a burnt offering instead of his son.*

At this point of my research, I was outraged. I asked things like *"What kind of sick game is this? Why do millions of people worship this horrible beast and call him righteous and holy?*

*And what about the psychological effects this must have had on Isaac?"* The poor boy was nearly murdered by his father, due to Yahweh's command! How would he ever trust another person? Is that what 'God' thinks of us—just tools to use and prove a point? (Apparently so, just read the book of Job).

It all comes down to greed and reward. Abraham later hears a promise from Heaven in verse 15 as a reward for hearing voices of angels and 'God,'and nearly murdering his child: *The angel of the Lord called to Abraham from Heaven a second time and said, "I swear by myself, declares the Lord, that because you have done this and have not withheld your son, your only son, I will surely bless you and make your descendants as numerous as the stars in the sky and as the sand on the seashore. Your descendants will take possession of the cities of their enemies, and through your offspring all nations on earth will be blessed, because you have obeyed me."*

So, the Bible teaches that an attempt at human sacrifice for the Christian god ends in reward for the attempted murderer. No wonder so many people on death row claim to be Christian! What would we do with Abraham today? 'Abrahams' are popping up all over, from women drowning their children, to a husband and father killing everyone and taking his own life due to hearing voices of angels, and claiming to be working with his god in a plot against evil. Abraham was no different, yet he was rewarded.

This obviously wasn't an isolated incident in the Bible, or in Yahweh's teachings. There are multiple stories involving the sacrifice of animals to Yahweh. The best I can gather, the archaic men running the religious world back then thought that if you burn something, it turns to smoke, and the smoke rises, so it must be reaching Heaven. They thought that by burning items they held as valuable, it was both a sacrifice of something they loved, plus Yahweh was getting the gift in the spiritual world by way of smoke.

Remember, this was the entire basis of the Cain and Abel rivalry and murder. Abel kept livestock and Cain harvested fruit. When it came time to give Yahweh the burnt offering, Abel placed his first-born sheep on the stone altar and set it on fire. The flames roared so they knew that Yahweh was pleased with the offering. Cain placed his fruit and vegetables on the altar, and the fire went out. Some Bibles simply say that Yahweh didn't respect Cain's offering but openly accepted Abel's. A book titled *Bible Stories for Children* (Horn, Cavanaugh, 1980) goes into grim detail about how the event took place, with the animal's fat "crackling" and Abel's gift being "pleasing to God" while Cain's grassy harvest created a "smoke, which choked out the flames" (16). This was taken to mean that Yahweh did not like Cain's fruit-based sacrifice because it wasn't as good as Abel's animal, so the fire went out. Cain later killed Abel out of jealousy and was punished by Yahweh as we all know. For many, this is an important story about jealousy. For me and my family, it is the first recorded story of a death in the name of religious beliefs.

Shouldn't someone have stopped to think that perhaps the fruit created a juice that put the fire out? Maybe the weeds that came with the grassy harvest dissipated the flames. There was no time for physics or reasonable thought in biblical stories. These were archaic, primitive, uneducated men making an attempt to explain science and the meaning of life, and failed miserably. It was all about teaching a lesson, that you'd better give your best and shed some blood for Yahweh's sake, or you simply weren't worthy of his love.

Among the more shocking stories, is the promise made by Jephthah in Judges 11:29–40. In short, he wanted to defeat the Ammorites, so he made a deal with Yahweh by saying *"If you will indeed deliver the people of Ammon into my hands, then it will be that whatever comes out of the doors of my house to meet me when I return in peace from the people of Ammon, shall surely be the Lord's, and I will offer it up as a burnt offering."* Yahweh makes good on the deal, Jephthah defeats the Ammorites in what the Bible calls " a very great slaughter," and as he returns home, his daughter comes out of his house dancing to meet him. After sending her away for two months, he kept his word and offered her up to Yahweh as a human sacrifice and 'burnt offering.' One thing's for sure: if the Christian god exists, he feels that the shedding of blood, animal, and more importantly, *human* sacrifice is a way to accomplish goals and make deals. Don't believe me? Just ask Jesus.

This was very disturbing to me. I was hoping to make sense of this through further research, but I was beginning to doubt the possibility of finding anything that could make these sacrifices tolerable.

## SINS vs. NATURE

Catholicism teaches that we are born sinners, innately evil and must repent and plead for 'God's' mercy. I began studying the logic behind instincts and trying to make a correlation with something all-powerful.

The definition of instinct is *an inborn pattern of behavior that is characteristic of a species and is often a response to specific environmental stimuli.* This means as humans, we are born with specific behaviors and reactions which help us respond to our surroundings. It's a natural process of responses. So as told by the religious faithful, the Christian god places rules against having feelings we are born with by his creation, in an effort to give us free will to disobey him.

It is a complete contradiction that the Christian god would purposely create you imperfectly as a sinner yet expects you to begin this impossible race against time to become perfect and repent before death. If you fail, the punishment is eternal fire. I don't know about you, but this is where I decided that I definitely wasn't Catholic.

Are you really okay with this logic? The Christian god created you as bad yet expects you to become good and repent before time runs out, or suffer an awful punishment. This sounds more like a horrible reality show that most of us would opt out of, given the chance. The request for repentance in itself is even ridiculous, as you are apologizing for being created as a sinner, which you had no say in. Where's the free will in that?

ɔle of this, it is considered wrong by the Christian ʯ man to have sexual thoughts about a woman he is not married to. Isn't this really just an attraction, which is usually required before reproduction in all creatures? Isn't this required to continue life? This is just an instinct which ensures the continuation of our species. Why would the Christian god say it's wrong if he placed this inborn characteristic within your genetic makeup? Is it a test? Is it tempting?

For another example, in the creationist belief, the Creator gave us the ability and intelligence to doubt *facts* yet instructs us not to doubt *him*. We are punished for not trusting in words written by other men (although we are told that all people are sinners), yet we are also punished for seeking knowledge, as Adam and Eve were for eating from the "Tree of Knowledge of Good and Evil."

What a conundrum! We can't find our own facts, because searching for knowledge in places other than Yahweh's word is wrong. We can't talk directly to Yahweh because he is omnipotent, and we are not worthy. We are not to question religious doctrine, or we are called infidels. Yet if we get it wrong in the end, we burn for eternity. What a concept of Holiness!

So how do we know how to live? Where do our morals come from? Are they really from the Christian god as we have been taught? Look at some instinctive 'sins' of other creatures, to view the Christian god's creation. Adult male gorillas sometimes kill their young to prevent leadership competition within the family. From the creationist perspective, is that not instinctive murder by Yahweh's creature? When the male mountain lion forcefully mates with a female by biting her and holding her down, is that not instinctive rape by Yahweh's creature? Ultimately, we are forced to feel bad for feelings the Creator allegedly forced us to have, yet we are held guilty even for our thoughts.

Why is it so hard to know the truth yet so important that we believe it without hard evidence? If the Christian god created all living things, where are the morals in animals? If this was such an 'intelligent design' why are we forced to suffer due to the actions of Adam and Eve? This is not fairness but could be called wrathful at best. By this point in my journey I was becoming increasingly frustrated by the lack of answers and the abundant flow of assumptions, excuses, and contradictions.

It seems if the Christian god exists he has given us an impossible task, with an atrocious punishment for life—and even more so for failure. I say all of these things not to mock Christianity, but to show you the evidence I've discovered on my journey toward Jesus Christ. The reality is that something of a divine makeup, as the Christian god would have to be, would not be limited to the contradictions of our world, nor would the Bible (if it were holy and divinely inspired) be limited to the scientific knowledge of the people at that time. In other words, we'd never have to make excuses by saying *"well that was back then,"* and *"in those days things were different,"* or *"he doesn't mean for us to do that now."* If the inspiration was timeless, it's only logical to think the instructions would be as well.

The Bible makes reference to the illegitimacy of being gay in many different ways. Matthew 19:4, Romans 1:26, Corinthians 6:9, and Timothy 1:8 all make claims against homosexuality. In fact, Leviticus 20:13 specifically says that gays should be killed!

I thought we were not allowed to murder… and that Yahweh is not the author of confusion, but I digress.

If being gay is so wrong, why is roughly 4% of our human population born attracted to the same sex? According to this same book, the Christian god created all of these people. Did he make a mistake? According to the Bible, that's impossible! He's the Christian god! That reasoning is equivalent to you baking a cake and then punishing that cake for not tasting as good as you hoped. Wouldn't that be your fault? Not if you were incapable of making an error. It's much easier to say "all cakes that I make are perfect, so if one comes out wrong; it must be punished because it is obviously tainted by evil." This is a ridiculous concept that reminds me of the Wizard of Oz screaming, "Pay no attention to the man behind the curtain!"

The Christian argument for this is that Yahweh tempts people in different ways. Before any evidence was presented that people are in fact born gay, Christian leaders said that gays were making a choice. Now that scientific evidence can prove a person is born gay due to a lack of brain exposure to male sex hormones prior to birth, those same leaders claim that Yahweh makes them that way as a temptation, and that each gay person should choose to fight those urges for 'God.' Before leaving this point, I must reference James 1:13, which tells us that the god of the Bible does not tempt anyone. That was a head scratcher for me, and hopefully it's one for the reader as well.

When discussing gay marriage, you really have to approach it from two sides—a basic humanist perspective and a legal perspective.

I will quickly explore both avenues. Let me start by saying that the federal Constitution doesn't mention the word 'marriage' once. It never states it is legal or illegal for people of the same sex to become married. It doesn't even define the word marriage. So for all those conservatives who want to leave our country as the fore-fathers meant it to be, why would you debate an action they left as legal? If they were against it, they would have written specifics; but they weren't. They were for the freedom of choice on many levels. Are you suggesting that you know better than the men that founded our country?

I'm looking into my red crystal ball for a moment, and I can see what all the conservatives are thinking: *"It was left up for the states to decide!"* Thank you for being so predictable. It was in fact left up to the states to define marriage and to decide not just who can marry but also common law terms and specific marriage rights. However, even in the ripe-red state of Texas, which is deep rooted with religious Republican ideology, there was no definition of the word marriage or article banning same sex marriage until 2005!

So from a legal and constitutional standpoint, using both federal and state statutes, there has been nothing illegal about gay marriage for hundreds of years. Yet thousands of gay people have been turned away from their partners in the hospital, denied insurance benefits, and treated as second-class citizens—just as blacks were treated when they were turned away from voting booths. How could we have allowed this for so long?

Despite the evidence and multiple tests that have been done, gays are typically viewed as if they have a choice in the matter.

Our society sees gay people as choosing to be different in an effort to stand out. Stop for a moment and think about that notion. As a straight person, could you force yourself to be attracted to someone of the same sex? Even if you could force yourself to be with them in some form even once under extreme duress, could you live everyday kissing that person against your will? Could you hold their hand in the park, or have a successful life together? Would it be worth it just to snub your nose at society? No, you couldn't; and I couldn't either. At some point, you would defect back to the opposite sex even if it were taboo, because that's what feels natural to you. Now, does that mean you are 'choosing' to like the opposite sex? Is that really a choice we have the capacity to make?

You simply can't force yourself to be attracted. We have to look at this physiologically. If it is impossible for you to choose the *same* sex against your nature, don't you think it's impossible for homosexuals to choose the *opposite*? There's just a fundamental difference in your brains; that's as far as it goes. Gay people have no more chosen to be gay than women have chosen to be female. One day, our government will see that, too. As for the votes in state legislature to ban gay marriage, I will say this: it's simply not fair to let the majority vote on how the minority is treated. You are putting it up for vote, to decide who should be discriminated against. That's like asking a bunch of slave owners if slavery should be abolished. It wasn't up to them; it took a war to make the decision. The right man got into office and made the best case for all Americans and our future as a country. Other laws, such as gun control in state legislations, regulate people who choose to participate by owning that gun. Gay people are not choosing to be who they are. Controlling them at that point is blatant discrimination because they are being treated differently due to things they cannot control. To prove this point, in mid-2009, a committee of the American Psychological Association released a study that said gay-straightening has not been shown to work, and the APA's Council of Representatives passed a resolution suggesting that professional counselors not offer therapy services to their patients, because being gay is not a disorder, or something one can fix. For those who claim we should let gays have Civil Unions but not call it marriage, I say you carry the same logic as those that failed miserably during the civil rights movement, which held a similar mentality that *Blacks can sit on the bus, they just can't sit here.*

Why isn't it a marriage if two people love one another—simply by definition? Those semantics should not be enough to divide our fellow Americans and deny them rights to be considered a married couple.

## THOU SHALT NOT KNOW

In any battle, the primary strategy of your enemy is to remove your fundamental needs, to take the resources you depend on for survival in an effort to destroy you from within. This is very effective and has worked in war for thousands of years. It's also why politicians run negative campaign ads. Their own positive message alone is not enough to persuade voters; they feel the need to destroy the other candidate's character so you will no longer listen to what he or she has to say. Again, by removing the resource of knowledge and communication, they have weakened their opponent in the eyes of the voter.

If the candidate has no voice, he is no competition. If the enemies have no resources, they are no threat. So what is the best defense against fear? Knowledge, and I've found that it's the primary resource religion wants to take from us. I understand, this is a pretty serious accusation, so I will explain myself carefully.

The Bible's description of Jehovah creating the Garden of Eden includes Genesis 2:9 *And out of the ground made the Lord, to grow every tree that is pleasant to the sight, and good for food; the tree of life also in the midst of the garden, and the tree of knowledge of good and evil.* It continues in Genesis 2:16-17 *And the Lord God commanded the man, saying, Of every tree of the garden thou mayest freely eat: But of the tree of the knowledge of good and evil, thou shalt not eat of it: for in the day that thou eatest thereof thou shalt surely die.* This is an amazing metaphor. If one eats from the tree of *knowledge*, they will surely die! Not only is this a great lesson learned about the punishments of attempting to obtain knowledge, but this very moment is noted by Christians to be the sole purpose we feel pain, shame, become sick, and need hospitals. We suffer on a daily basis all due to the fact that Adam and Eve attempted to obtain knowledge! No wonder we are afraid to question Christianity! No wonder books like mine are so rare in comparison to those that praise Jesus! We have learned these stories since we were children, forced to go to Bible Study and Sunday school.

It was becoming very clear to me what was being portrayed here. The Bible wants you to shun logical facts, be afraid of knowledge, and be afraid of free thought and reasonable logic. Religion wants you to turn over your right of thinking and questioning, in an effort to control you and lead the masses in a specific direction to fulfill their leaders' agendas.

Now let me propose this question to you: If you really believed in your stance on an issue, and wanted me to join you in the fight, wouldn't you encourage me to go obtain whatever knowledge I could on the topic? If it were truly a good cause, and justification for a resolution to a problem plaguing our society, would you not welcome research? As with any politician or religious leader, you would only want to hide the facts that could be detrimental to your agenda. What agenda does religion have? The answer is *power*, also known as 10% of your income and world-wide political and territorial influence. Of course they want *all* the power, and that means taking it from you in the form of knowledge.

I was beginning to discover that they wanted me to know nothing, and believe everything. I refused and continued asking questions in disbelief that more people hadn't done the same before me.

# CHAPTER 4: INVESTIGATING ATHEISM

# READING INTO REASON

Upon researching different religions and reading multiple books by former Atheists turned Christians, and *vice-versa*, I was tirelessly looking for something that made sense to me and that I could relate to. During one particular search online, I came across the *American Atheists* Web-site. I found an article written by a man named Frank R. Zindler and was absolutely overcome with a sense of relief. The feeling I had must be similar to what a boy raised by wolves would feel like upon finally seeing another human! Every word I read made perfect sense to me. With each click, I visited a new section of the site which connected with another part of my secular life and arguments against religions. I had worded some of these things in my own uneducated way, but here was a former professor of biology, and man who could speak the original languages of the Bible, saying the same things and even more, with detailed evidence to back it up! I had never read the writings of someone that knew so much about the Bible, and still disagreed with it. All the things I had wanted to say were being said! There was someone else out there standing up against the atrocities religions were causing, and it felt great to witness it. Not only was this educated man debating Christians publically, but he had a whole team of people who felt exactly like I did all working together as activists for causes such as gay rights, the separation of church and state, and the rights of non-religious people to live peacefully. I was very excited, and couldn't help but read more.

All the imponderables I had about religions (and Christianity in particular) began to make sense when I applied the answers of Atheism.

**How could one religion such as 'Baptists' know they had it right for sure?** They couldn't, because there are no right answers on how to worship 'God' because one doesn't exist. That's why religions battle one another. As comedian Richard Jeni once said, *"You're all basically killing each other to see who has the better imaginary friend."*

**Why does every religion think they have it right?** Religious books are left up to interpretation and do not have an omniscient inspiration. This means it's left up to the leaders of that society to interpret the holy books in a way which conforms the people to the rules they wish to enforce.

**Why did early Christians believe a fiery Hell was underground?** Most likely, the ascension of lava through ground cracks and explosions from volcanoes gave way to a myth of a steaming hot underworld, and many religions boast of an amazing after life, while Christianity's selling point is more along the lines of the threat of Hell, which is basically saying the same thing in different words, as Christopher Hitchens put's it in *God is Not Great: How Religion Poisons Everything* (2007).

**Why are innocent children born with deformities?** No god exists, and it's simply a flaw in human genetics and embryology that scientists are working to correct. These things happen at the same statistical rates to people of all cultures and religions, and prayer has no affect on these disorders.

**If 'God' blesses America, why doesn't he heal injured soldiers who have fought for his special country?** Because no god exists, but everyone wants to feel as though they have a mightier power on their side, so they assign a metaphysical spirit to watch over them. Soldiers who are injured and die for our country are to be respected and hailed as heroes, but no god should be given credit for any battle won or lost.

**Was Jesus the son or the god?** The reason this one was so difficult is because the answer is neither! The story of Jesus being the embodiment of a godhead, was copied from older religions and beliefs as I've previously mentioned.

**Why do so many people believe it if it's not true?** Sociology, group psychology, family pressure, rituals, comfort, and early indoctrination are all reasons why religions continue to flourish. By the time people are old enough or educated enough to think for themselves, their religion is so ingrained in them, it's nearly impossible to have a free thought without the possibility of a god existing. This is also why most people share similar belief systems of their parents.

**Why do so many people reject evolution?** It's simply easier to repeat what other people say than to do our own research. We *listen* better than we *read* and we *repeat* better than we *think*.

Finally, everything made sense. The answers I had been looking for were not there, and that's why they were so hard to find! Placing the answer of a god to any of those questions only begs more questions, but does not provide answers we can comprehend with normal logic.

# EVOLUTION

Evolution is often misunderstood and misquoted, so I'd like to take a moment to clear it up. I really do mean just a moment, especially in comparison with some of the extremely detailed evidential works out there, namely Richard Dawkins' *The Greatest Show on Earth* (2009). The book is well worth the money, even if you only read Chapters 7 and 11, which specifically deal with the evolution of man. Dawkins provides amazing details (more so than many biology text books I've encountered) on the specific and undeniable facts of evolution. One cannot simply read those two chapters and still believe in the creation story of Genesis (not without throwing logic out the window, of course).

Creationists often develop straw-man arguments to put into the mouths of evolutionists, implying that they think that at one point in time, two apes mated and created a human, or that humans 'descended' from present-day apes, monkeys, or other creepy crawly animals. Then, they charge evolutionists with defending those preposterous hypotheses, which of course is impossible. I can understand how that would be confusing if you don't have a clear understanding of evolution. When I am presented with the question of "When did the first human arrive, and what were its parents?" I simply respond by saying "What's a human?" This isn't sarcasm; it's a naturalist investigator asking for a realistic answer.

You see, evolution doesn't claim that humans were born from monkeys as most Creationists will have you think—the claim is that all living things have a common ancestor somewhere down the line (that can be further explained by viewing a chart of the evolutionary tree). That is a huge difference! It's not fair to challenge the evolutionist to look back in time and ascertain what two creatures created the first human, or duck, or goat. Even if he was standing there during conception, he wouldn't know the answer! As an illustration, what would you call something that was 98.9% chicken and 1.1% hawk? You'd probably call it a chicken. It may look different than most chickens, but you wouldn't rule it out of being a chicken because of a slight difference in appearance. Think of how dogs are categorized when breeds mix. Many times, a dog has so many different breeds in its blood line, it's referred to as a mutt. But is it still a dog? Of course it is. This is where the lines become very fuzzy, and without scientifically studying the genetic makeup of each creature, it's impossible to know what to call it. That's what zoologists and anthropologists do with animals and humans respectively.

There was obviously a time period in which 'humans' were in the same condition—certain portions of evolution, especially the upright-walking human variation, take an incredibly long amount of time to show obvious changes, and it never stops adapting. In fact, humans aren't done evolving even today, nor will we ever be.

So many creationists assert that there is not enough evidence, or that there are missing links, or that very few fossils have actually been found. Then, they tend to just repeat that same thing over and over, even in the media until millions of people believe it. Surprisingly, it's so common, that when I begin to debate creationists, they don't even bother looking into the scientific history on evolution, because they feel like they already have a good understanding of what it is. I hear things like *"you have your facts and I have my facts, we just trust different books!"* It's frustrating to say the least, because these people have never actually researched evolution. They simply believe what the average person says about it, and move on. Moreover, they consider the Bible to be fact and books on anthropology to be Atheist rhetoric. It's sad that so many people intentionally choose ignorance. They just won't look into it—probably out of a fear for being wrong. Once you see it, you simply can't deny the evidence.

I won't go into intricate details, as it has hopefully been clear that my goal was not to turn this into a text book—but I will give you just a few terms to research on your own: *Australopithecus | Homo habilis | Homo erectus | Homo antecessor | Homo heidelbergensis | Homo sapiens | anthropology | natural selection.*

Read up on those for just a few minutes, and then read the Genesis account of creation and try not to feel silly. Just having a peek into this world of science and reviewing the fossils that are available to us will really open your mind to the absurdities within the creation stories. Let me be clear: books on anthropology or evolution are not simply 'another account' of our presence on earth, or 'an attempt' to find out how we got here. These are not 'my facts' that are separate but equal to the 'facts' of the Bible. *The fossil record is a fact that stands alone.* It's very real, and you can go see it (or at least casts of the originals) in any serious museum in your area. The assertions in the Bible cannot be tested. We do not have a preserved ark, or DNA from Jesus proving his divinity, and the metaphysical claims within the stories of creation are not physiologically possible. You simply can't have trees, plants, or light without the sun. Man wasn't made from 'dust,' and a woman wasn't 'fashioned out of a rib.' The 'facts' of the Bible are akin to the 'facts' within the Qur'an, or the Holy Vedas, and should be treated as the mythology they so rightly are. Religions should only be compared to other religions, but never to scientific fact.

In a video sent to me by a preacher friend of mine, a Christian scientist appears on screen and discusses the theory we've all heard: *"Intelligent design needs a designer."* He claims to *"scientifically prove"* how intricate, majestic, and perfect nature is, and couldn't have possibly been an accident in space. Therein lies the proof that the Christian god created the universe and all nature therein. Well, isn't that convenient? It's too perfect to be an accident! In his opinion, and that of many creationists, similarities in design and the beautiful nature as it exists are all enough proof that the Christian god created everything, and he is indeed perfect. So let's have a closer look at this perfect design.

The Bible states that the Christian god gave man dominion over Earth and all that creeps or dwells within earth. Yet, Earth is made up of 71% water, which man cannot inhabit or consume for life. That leaves only 29% of earth as land, for man. However, much of that land is too cold for man to dwell, and other places are simply too hot and dry. In addition, thousands of miles of soil and desert sand cannot produce food, and billions of gallons of water in the oceans cannot be drunk. Our planet is mostly liquid, yet every summer I have to conserve water or I will get a ticket from the city! What a design! I suppose I could build you a church that was roughly 20% useful, and you would consider me an intelligent designer!

To top it off, the human eye can't see in the dark, yet half of our time on earth as it was 'designed' is spent in darkness. Speaking of intelligent, how awesome are hailstorms, hurricanes, typhoons, earthquakes, and tornadoes? They couldn't be more perfectly designed for man's natural need to survive! However, since the Christian god can't make a mistake, Christian apologists use these disasters to say, "God isn't happy with the way we are living," or more arrogantly, "God has a plan, and these disasters will turn more people toward Christ." What a trade off: 200,000 dead humans for a few baptisms! Does that sound fair? These apologists have a wonderful knack for scaring folks into believing. I know, because I was once terrified.

Animals are designed to procreate. So why would an intelligent designer make it nearly impossible? Male lions actually attract females by having a darker mane. Yet scientific studies have proven that males with darker manes have a higher concentration of abnormal sperm. Also, male guppies attract females by having bright colors and big flashy spots. This also attracts predators, and many male guppies are often eaten before they are able to mate at all. As a side note, you must know that Richard Dawkins details a specific experiment with guppies in the book mentioned above, in which a scientist was able to coerce evolution in that species in just two years! It's an amazing testament to evolution and is a must read. Now back to our wonderful process of intelligently-designed procreation.

The sage-grouse male attracts females by inflating and releasing the giant air sacks in its chest. This sound can be heard for more than three miles away and is also responsible for male sagegrouses being eaten at twice the rate of females because it also attracts predators. In fact, females outnumber males approximately two-to-one in the sage-grouse community! The male babirusa is a pig-like animal that has large teeth growing upwards through its snout. If these are trimmed back or broken, the male will almost never find a mate, because the females see that as a sign of being sickly or weak. The long, strong, and fully developed bones are what really gets the girls! However, if the large bones go untouched (and therefore grow perfectly according to the intelligent design), they will actually curve back and grow into the animal's brain, killing him! These do not sound like perfect designs! However, they do sound like malformations within evolution that will eventually correct themselves through natural selection.

Creationists also say evolution in nature is not evident in today's world, because there are no hybrid species of animals. Kirk Cameron once brought this point forth in a televised debate against Atheists, as he held up cartoon-like drawings of fictional animals such as a "croco-duck" to make a mockery of evolution. This is quite sad. While it got a laugh at the debate, many people felt sorry for Cameron because his ignorance really shined through. He has apparently failed to do the research needed for a debate against evolution. I'm not sure what research could be done, however. I suppose it would be similar to that of one who wishes to deny that babies are born and tries to present evidence of the 'Stork Theory,' as Dawkins often jokes. Cameron can only make irrational assertions and claim that any missing evidence is the result of a godly power that we can't possibly understand. This is known as the 'God of the Gaps' argument.

What would a *transitional* animal really look like in today's world? Of course it wouldn't have the body of a duck with crocodile teeth, but it would show some resemblance to at least two animals. If something existed in modern times that was proven to be related to two modern species, would that change your mind about evolution?

Well let's start there: have you ever seen a snake blink? Probably not, considering the fact that traditional snakes don't have eye lids. So the chances are, if you *did* see a snake blink, it would probably be a legless lizard referred to as the glass snake. It appears to be the perfect transition between a lizard and a snake. Its tiny hind legs are almost invisible as it slithers across the ground, but it lacks the expandable jaws of true snakes, and its eyes are unmistakable for those of lizards. But there are no living transitional animals so to speak—the glass snake simply shares an ancestor with both snakes and other lizards—it's not a direct descendent from either of them.

The mudskipper is a phenomenal animal! This fish actually comes out of the water and walks across dry land, rocks, and mud, to get to the next body of water. Please research this remarkable creature, and you will surely have another look at natural selection. There are several species of birds that currently have wings and are obviously in the bird family, but cannot fly. The extreme birds such as penguins actually prefer to swim rather than walk. Their wings have developed very flipper-like characteristics, yet they are still classified as birds. Moreover, there are flying birds that actually dive up to one-hundred feet under water to catch food, and then swim (or float) back to the surface. How could that possibly happen? Ask Kirk Cameron, and I'm sure you'll find that it's only by the grace of his god.

The undeniable resemblance of animals is yet another strong clue pointing towards evolution. As my good friend the preacher stated, this is only evidence of similarities in design by the same designer. I agree to a point, we just disagree on exactly what that designer was. My first question would be what's the point? Why make an alligator and a crocodile and have Adam name them each something different? Why are there thousands of different types of birds; why not just one bird? What's the need for over 3,000 different types of lizards? Why do we share 98% of our genes with apes? If the Christian god created us to be similar, why would he copy the same errors and flaws in our human bodies that are apparent in apes?

My layman's statement on evolution is this: We have facts to support it, and even if we didn't, it is simply more feasible to think that several species had one common ancestor than to believe a magical being created everything we know of in six days. Is this really an intelligent design?

## AVERAGE AMERICAN MORALS

It's important to stop and think before you claim to have Christian morals and be sure you fully understand what that means. The average American may claim Christian morality, as if that holds a higher standard than humanistic ethics—yet they will walk out of a store knowing they have been undercharged without telling the clerk. If you believe in the Bible, and have read it, then you know of a wrathful god that punishes mercilessly. Yet, you choose to ignore that on Saturday nights because there are no immediate effects of your negative behavior. The Christian god doesn't appear before you and "smite thee," therefore you think you are getting away with something or that your 'personal relationship' allows you to bend the rules. The Christian god is not described as a tolerant preschool teacher; he is described as a vengeful, jealous god. So why would you test the waters if you truly believed that book?

Ask yourself: do I really believe the entire Bible is true? If yes, then why don't you live according to Matthew 7:21? If you believe it to be true in your heart, why aren't you doing everything you can to be absolutely sure you will enter Heaven, including obeying the 'will of God?' If you are a preacher, or consider yourself a 'person of God,' you still sin on a regular basis, but why? Dare you blame it on your god for creating you as a sinner?

The point here is that according to the Bible, it is nearly impossible to enter Heaven. Luke 13:23-24 tells us: *"Then said one unto him, Lord, are there few that be saved? And he said unto them, Strive to enter in at the strait gate: for many, I say unto you, will seek to enter in, and shall not be able."*

In order to trust the Bible on its interpretation of where we are all going when we die, or the actions it requires from us to get there, we must also be able to trust it on where we've been. This means looking at this book as history and fact. In order to do that, we must check the Bible's credit. Frank Zindler said it best in his debate on the great flood, when he noted the amount of rain that must have fallen in order for the account of Noah's Ark in the Bible to be true. He mentioned the amount of rain that would be necessary to fulfill the story would have also been enough fresh water to dilute the salt water in the oceans to the point of which marine life would not be able to live. In the story of Noah's Ark, it specifically says that Noah was instructed to fill his boat with land-dwelling animals.

This was obviously before the writer of the story understood that rain water and salt water were not the same. If the Christian god were interested in saving the lives of animals, he would have instructed Noah to take aboard marine life as well, to preserve the species. Leaving marine life in the ocean would mean certain death because of the dilution of salt water by the fresh rain water.

The story also mentions that "birds and small creeping things" were included on the ark. The ark was made of wood. Were woodpeckers and termites included on this voyage? Just think about that one and then visit the American Atheists Web-site for a full text of the actual debate between two biologists, one Atheist, one Christian. It's truly a remarkable look into reasoning. The Bible is full of stories like this, which causes questions of its validity. For example, in Numbers 22:28, it states *the Lord opened the mouth of a donkey* and it spoke to a man named Balaam for a full conversation. The donkey actually speaks at least three sentences to the man. In Genesis, if you remember, it was a serpent that spoke to Eve and convinced her to eat the fruit. These stories are not taught as metaphors or Christian folklore; this is recognized as religious doctrine. You absolutely must question stories like this—especially from a book that is describing to you the most important decision of your life. The facts in this book are supposed to discern where you will spend eternity. Yet, we are not supposed to question it?

The entire purpose of this chapter is for Christians to realize the ridiculous predicament the Bible says they are in. There is no way one would expect you to be born a sinner against your will, then begin this impossible race to perfection before your death. To expect such a feat would be ridiculous.

# EXPLANATIONS AND APOLOGISTS

As with any powerful system, there are people involved with Christianity who will defend their cause to the end. Instead of looking back at their leader (godhead), historicity, and questioning authority, they will make every possible excuse for that authority to justify the group's actions. In the religious world, these people are called apologists. There are even Bachelors and Masters Degrees that can be obtained in 'Apologetics' for just about every denomination of Christianity. There are people called Christian apologists ready to answer many of the questions I've asked and put their own spin on just about every question that could be raised.

Through my research, I've had discussions and debates with many apologists, and I have to say, these people are very good at what they do. They have been trained well and will often only debate in a setting which allows them either control of the conversation (like a radio show where they can disconnect at any time) or within the walls of a church where they have an advantage (in which they can use jokes or quick come-backs to have the crowd laughing at their opponent).

Many preachers are apologists-in-training. Basically, you can think of them as Spin Doctors who can put just about any spin on a question you ask to make it fit within their Christian view. Apologists also have a few safety nets for when you ask difficult questions or when you ask a question they've never heard. As I walked through looking for real answers on Christianity, in an effort to be a better Christian, I became extremely frustrated by these tactics, because I wanted answers, not politics.

For example, if the question is about something horrible or outrageous that Jesus or Yahweh commanded, like a graphic death or sacrifice, the apologists will file it under 'hyperbole,' which is just an exaggeration to prove a point. They may say *"Well, Jesus didn't mean to actually hate your father, that's just hyperbole for making the point that you must be willing to do anything for Jesus."* However, when it's convenient for the words to be taken literally, such as Jesus holding bread and saying "This is my body," the Catholics create an entire belief system from that. I began to notice that Christians will change their position and subjective interpretation of the Bible to fit whatever life-style they were raised to live.

Another example is when we ask questions regarding the limitations of Yahweh. *"Why doesn't he stop evil?" "Is he powerful enough to overcome birth control, or prevent abortion?"* These types of questions usually receive a response that Yahweh intentionally dilutes his own power to give us free will. This is the ultimate catch-all for explaining why the Christian god appears to have human weaknesses and godly powers which would be a contradiction in most logical situations.

The final canned answer of Christian apologists is that our tiny human minds just can't understand godly methods. We've heard *"God works in mysterious ways."* That's really just an excuse for not having an answer.

Ultimately, if you are ever able to ask apologists a question they have not been asked before, or one that does not quite fall into a category of which they have a canned answer, they will simply reword the question for you, in such a way that it falls into a category they can defend. You may hear them say *"I think what you're trying to say is..."* At that point, you can trust they will simplify your question to fall into a category they can handle.

As an example, I once asked a Christian apologist, who has a PhD in philosophy, my question about the alleged sacrifice of Jesus. To reiterate, I didn't understand how we could consider that 'God' *sacrificed* his son, when he still has him by his side in the Christian belief. His response was that I was proving the problem of evil to be an invalid argument, by saying that Heaven is so amazing, death isn't that bad!

Do you see what happened here? He didn't answer the question—he redirected it to something he could handle. That's why I call them Spin Doctors. I was not conceding a belief in Heaven by wording my question that way, I was merely pointing out a contradiction in the belief. Without ever answering my question, he managed to avoid the embarrassment of not knowing how to respond, and at the same time, made me look as though I had proved his point for him. This impressed many people, but not me. He pulled the wool right over their eyes; but I suppose that's only natural for a flock of sheep.

An even more extreme case of apologetics would be found at a popular Baptist church in Dallas, Texas that encourages gays to join their congregation. When challenged about the portions of the Bible that condemn homosexuality, their response is that *those* verses are referring to straight men who lie with other men, not men that were *born* gay. What a spin! Just as I've said before, one can make the Bible say just about anything, which makes it begin to appear quite useless a credible source for anything.

Keep these things in mind as you ask religious leaders the questions that are important to you. Don't let them avoid the question or reword it for you. Be very direct and keep your question as short as possible, to minimize the amount of word-play they can use. Remember, the point is not to disprove but to receive explanations and then decide if that reasoning is logical.

## FAIRNESS: A QUICK THOUGHT

Let's say I'm giving both of my children important tasks. I go to my son and tell him directly, exactly what I need done. He immediately fails to complete the task correctly.

Then, for my daughter's task, I tell my Hispanic friend what I want her to do, and he writes down the instructions in Spanish. I then mail that letter to Korea and have them translate it. It is then typed by a translator in Korean and sent to the Queen of England who re-words her own version in English. This is called the "Queen Elizabeth Version" of my instructions. She prints the document and holds it for 25 years. At the end of the holding period, she mails the document to my daughter who must follow the instructions. My daughter fails to complete the task correctly.

Should both children be equally blamed and punished for not completing their tasks as I instructed? I don't believe a holy being would plan things so that it would become increasingly more difficult as time passes for a person to successfully follow the path before them.

If you think my analogy was unfair, spanning twenty-five years and a few translators, think now about the Bible, written over a period of sixteen hundred years, in three different languages, by forty different authors, and edited by thousands of unknown scribes, resulting in many different English versions. It should not depend on the successful translation of other humans. It should not depend on another's interpretations of the words. I should know it to be truth and have a choice to accept it or turn away from it. As it stands today, Christians only hope, trust, and believe it to be true. Life is just too important to rest on such intangible feelings, and this same instruction book tells us that the god depicted therein is not the author of confusion!

After all the research I had done, my conclusion wasn't very difficult. I started this journey to find 'God,' and what I found were more gods. I began looking for the perfect religion, and what I found were more religions. I searched for the meaning of life, and I found it is what we make it. Most of all, no religious doctrine had proven itself to be the truth, but only more confusing. I finally decided, I was an Atheist. There is no magic, there are no spirits, and I live without guilt every day. What I've found most of all in my search *for* religious perfection, is freedom *from* it.

## THE FAITH-O-METER THEORY

One of the stronger arguments against Atheism is not made by religious folks at all, but often times by the Agnostics, who claim Atheism requires just as much faith as religion. The basis of their argument is that the separation of Atheism and Agnosticism basically comes down to Atheists having faith that there is no god, while Agnostics stand firm on the notion that Atheists and theists alike are attempting to resolve the unattainable. To further this argument, during a religious debate, a Christian once said to me, *"I don't have enough faith to be an Atheist!"* This claim comes from the many religious folks who assert being an Atheist requires persons to have all knowledge of the universe in order to firmly state that there are no gods. Of course, being that we all lack that knowledge, the claim is sometimes made that Atheists must have a tremendous amount of faith—even more so than theists. These postulations come from both ends of our debate spectrum, so I feel it's necessary to address them here.

First of all, as with any good discussion, we must speak the same language. I will not accept 'faith' as only a religious term. The word actually derives from the Latin *fidere,* meaning 'to trust' which is akin to *fides,* also meaning 'promise, loyal, and assurance.' This is how we adopted the phrase *bona fide* meaning 'real' or 'factual,' and 'fidelity' meaning 'loyalty' and 'sincerity.' Webster has three English definitions for *faith*, the first being *'an allegiance to a duty or person, and sincerity of intentions.'* This is used when stating a person is 'faithful' to his or her spouse. The second version of the word is wholly dedicated to belief in a god, so we can quickly rule that one out for Atheists. The final definition simply states *'complete trust, especially with strong conviction.'* Atheists We do trust evidence and science. It is impossible to say Atheists have no conviction at all, but it's more accurate to say that Atheists have confidence in their process of forming knowledge, because it's been rewarded in the past, multiple times over, and in a controlled environment.

A preacher once told me, *"You would be a great Christian if you ever started to believe; we could use your level of conviction in our church!"* He followed by saying, *"I have to say, I respect you for having so much determination to stand up for what you believe in."* I responded with, *"Correction—I stand up to what I don't believe in."* That statement sets the tone that we Atheists do not profess a system of beliefs that requires the burden of proof. It is the duty of accusers to prove the existence of *their* gods, and we only stand up to them when they use their religious agendas to infringe on the civil liberties of others, or assert their beliefs as fact or common knowledge without adequate proof. This is where the problem comes in. What may be proof to one may not be proof to another; so what is the meaning of proof?

Imagine for a moment that faith and evidence are measured by fluid and space in a single tube (such as a thermometer). The fluid represents the amount of evidence available. As it rises, one comes closer to a full confirmation (proof). Any remaining space in the tube is a lack of evidence, also known as faith. Of course, upon discovering all possible evidence, the tube is full because faith is no longer needed. I call this the *Faith-o-meter Theory*, and it concludes that the greatest assumption, with the least amount of evidence, must have the largest amount of faith.

In the simplest form of examining this theory, let's set the scenario that Beth is standing in front of a closed door. By stating that she believes a dog is behind the door, she is making that statement on 100% faith, because she has no evidence to support that claim (her Faith-o-meter is empty). Once she hears a dog bark-ing, her evidence rises to approximately 50%, because she must concede that while she's fairly certain the barking is coming from behind the door, the audio she hears could be a recording, or the dog could be in an adjacent room. Her statement is then made up of 50% evidence and 50% faith. If she were to open the door and find an actual dog (not just a hallucination), her evidence would rise to 100% because she would have effectively proven her faith and confirmed the existence of the dog. This would be the ultimate proof. However, with only partial evidence, and the possibilities of fallacies lingering, she must rely on a great deal of faith to make the claim that a dog is behind the door prior to knowing it to be true.

In a slightly more ambiguous form, you may have faith that your mother gave birth to you—so you go to the hospital where you were allegedly born and check the records. Sure enough, your mother's name is next to yours, and the documents provide you with a substantial amount of evidence for your Faith-o-meter. But is that really absolute proof? Should your Faith-o-meter be at 100%? The documents could have been mis-typed, or you could have been unintentionally switched at birth and given the name of the child that was set to go home with your mother. Even with this document as evidence, there is a slight chance of error. Therefore, while you may wholeheartedly believe your mother gave birth to you, 100% of the evidence has not been obtained; therefore, even though your Faith-o-meter has a substantial amount of evidence, say 98%, you are still relying on a small percentage of faith—but still, it is faith.

With a full understanding of both aforementioned scenarios, do you think it is fair to make the claim that you and Beth have just as much faith? When she *believes* there is a dog barking prior to discovering evidence, is that *hope* just as much evidence as your birth certificate? Of course not—simply because you personally deem proof to be only that which satisfies your particular doubts. Therefore, if you do not have enough information, or even a problem complicated enough to form more detailed inquisitions, your doubts will be limited and therefore require less evidence before you consider it proof (your knowledge on the topic determines the size of your Faith-o-meter which needs filling).

We must remember that all seas are at the same level, regardless of depth. On the surface, they appear to be the same—but once you're in the water, the bottom can mean all the difference in the world! Simply because two people have faith, it doesn't make them equally blind to facts, and it doesn't mean that faith always means the same thing. Faith can be both justifiable and unjustifiable, and again, that justifiable faith should be more accurately referred to as confidence. However, that doesn't mean just because one has confidence, they are sure to be right. Some people have confidence out of ignorance, and simply don't know enough to doubt!

We find a great comparison with the deep-sea fisherman and scientists, who prior to 2004, had recovered the *bodies* of giant squid but had neither filmed nor captured one living. However, they had *confidence* that some were still out there. You may refer to this as justifiable faith, but again, it would more accurately be called an *inference* or *conclusion* based on evidence they had discovered. It would completely discount their records and research to say they had the same faith as the believers of Demeter, the Greek Goddess of Agriculture! That belief was obviously unjustified and therefore required large amounts of faith, much larger than the hope or trust that the fisherman once had.

Since we Atheists do not have all the answers, some level of confidence in our method of acquiring evidence is required, in the literal sense—just as the scientists looking for the giant squid trusted there was one living before it was proven. But pointing back to the Faith-o-meter Theory, when a greater amount of knowledge is discovered, a smaller amount of confidence (or faith in the literal sense) is required.

In addition, it is a much greater assumption to say a magical god exists and is intervening in human lives on earth than it is to state no such magic is possible. In fact, one statement is sensible and rational, and the other is a far-fetched claim that requires substantial amounts of faith. Perhaps it is fair to say the theist must have all knowledge of the universe in order to claim their god is the only god! Most Christians would probably argue that as fact, but biblically, Yahweh even mentions 'showing off' for other gods in the Old Testament. It is for reasons like this that a theist has the burden of proof with such an outstanding profession of faith that their religion is the only true one, with so much evident contradiction. The other type of faith simply lies in the falsehoods of others. The Atheist has not made a single claim, except that all supernatural claims are without proof.

If I were to try to be an Agnostic and say, *"I just don't know if there is a god,"* I would feel just as silly as saying *"I just don't know if there is a Tooth Fairy."* It's not so much that we Atheists have 'faith' in the lack of gods, but we do have confidence that theists accept fallacies as proof, most likely out of fear. This may be the same reason Agnostics will not profess true Atheism (the fear of being wrong), which is also self-defeating because without a stance one can never be right either! In the literal sense of trusting in evidence, I can't be a *faithful* Atheist, because I'm not *full* of faith. My lack of evidence for what I assert is nowhere near the amount of unjustifiable faith required to believe in magical spirits helping us with daily activities. But am I a *confident* Atheist? Yes.

# WHY DO ATHEISTS CARE?

As an Atheist, I often hear *"Why do you care about fighting against religion? Why do you care if I believe or not? Why would you want me to stop believing if it makes me happy?"*

The company you keep is very important to your success, and your past is quite often a reflection of your future. To be around people who are on drugs would bother you, because you feel it's a misleading lifestyle. I feel the same about religion. It is a mental drug, which has been made to appear as a good thing, when in fact it's a secret form of self-induced brainwashing.

The leaders of religion use fear to get you into church because the more members they have, the more money they collect at offering. You have a desire to believe in the gospels out of fear of going to Hell. You want to feel as though there is a savior or a way out. It makes life much easier to deal with while you're here.

I understand all of these emotions, because I was a believer, too. However, I must tell you, my sense of the urgency of life is now ten-fold greater since I no longer believe in Heaven. This life is all I have. This is my chance to make a difference. I don't believe I will ever be able to do good for others as an angel in an afterlife. Therefore, *now* is my time to be an angel looking over those around me. *Now* is my time to be a guardian for those that need protection. *Now* is my time to create Heaven for as many people as possible. So why do I care that you follow a religion?

The belief in a deity, afterlife, or any religion, basically comes with a sense of 'second chance' that doesn't exist. As a believer, you seem to be 'at peace' with failing at certain things, because this is just earth, and Heaven is the real eternal place of life. You see this life as a practice run of sorts. You tend to make excuses for your mistakes and hushing others by saying, *"Only God can judge me."* If there's a major decision to be made, you place it in your god's hands instead of controlling your own destiny. You wonder if things are meant to be instead of making them so. You feel like as long as you reach Heaven, you can start making a difference then, so you wait. Well, I'm not waiting.

If the entire world felt like there was no Heaven, and promised themselves to create a Heaven on earth, and promised to become a *guardian angel* now, the world would be a much better place. Things like this wouldn't be posted in our headlines: 13 YEAR OLD GIRL STONED TO DEATH AFTER BEING RAPED: After burying the child from the neck down, a man casting stones at her head for the Somalia Government said *"We will do what Allah has instructed us."* This is why I care.

The first section of the first chapter of this book is titled "I Wanted to Believe." I no longer do. It's not a choice I'm making, it's more of a sadness for what a god could actually be like if one did exist, watching the level of torment, sacrifice, and wars fought in his or her name without ever stopping the madness to clear things up. To think about something watching, with the powers to cure all the bad things yet choosing not to, churns my stomach. So many innocent lives have been lost, so many families have been ripped apart, so much has happened without a single hint of who is right or wrong, and it only seems to perpetuate the anxiety. Moreover, if that god were found to be of the Christian variation, commanding those innocent human deaths and sacrifices of animals to please his own ego—I would shudder at the site of how meager this god must be with such a low self-esteem. To have the need of being constantly praised, believed, and bowed to is such a sign of insecurity, I could hardly place any faith in such a leader—even 'knowing' of his existence. In fact, I'm confident that if I were to ever find myself face to face with such a deity, by the time I challenged his actions verses his words, and his chosen people verses their atrocities in his name, he would have a hard time believing in himself!

# CHAPTER 5: OUR SOCIETY

# A CHRISTIAN NATION

Do we deserve what's happening to us because, as a nation, we are shunning the Christian god? Many of you say the financial crisis we are facing right now is because we have removed your god from everything. Many more say this seemingly endless war is also due to the lack of 'God' in our lives. I see comments such as *"We are pushing him out of our lives."— We are taking him out of our court houses."—"What do you expect him to do?"*

I actually heard a woman interviewed shortly after a deadly school shooting who said, *"Well, we've taken God out of our schools, so he wasn't there to protect our children."* I suppose her perception has become her reality, but it has also become something other than Christianity. Allegedly, the Christian world view is that its god is everywhere, so how could we ever be without him? Again, these are the human limitations placed on Yahweh by Christians to help prove a point, as if a statute or regulation could keep at bay the most powerful being in the universe.

As for the Christian god being removed from our lives, I must address that by noting, my children are told to say *"One nation, Under God"* every morning in public school. So 'God' is still there. In court, I was forced to raise my right hand and swear to tell the whole truth, "So help me, God," and no one asked my religion first. He is still there, too. Every piece of money I spend says "In God We Trust" on it. He even lives in the wallets and purses of Muslims and Agnostics all over America. Each time I sneeze, someone says "God Bless You." I understand they are just being polite, so I simply thank them and move on, but would that be considered tolerance, or acceptance? How do they know if I am Christian or not? I don't believe they care. I simply say "thank you" because I don't have the time to explain to them that saying 'bless you' simply came from the fact that the Latin term 'spiritus' was the word for 'breath,' and when someone sneezed, their breath was forced out of them, so the rumor began that one must be 'blessed' before an evil 'spirit' entered the body (Zindler, 1985).

These points are brought up to prove that my children cannot get an education, I cannot handle legal matters, my family cannot purchase a single item with cash, and we can't even sneeze in public without bringing 'God' into our lives—at least on some level! Yet some Christians say our country deserves these horrible things that are happening in our culture because we have removed their god. Have we?

The assumption of 'God' is so ingrained in our society; it has been placed on our money and adopted by our government—even though our rights are supposed to defend us from that. So many people claim that we live in a Christian nation, but looking into the facts tells us a different story. We do not live in a Christian nation; we proudly live in a free country without an establishment of religion, with many of us choosing to be Christians.

In Article 11 of the Treaty of Tripoli on June 7, 1797, it was written, and later verbally confirmed by U.S. officials that: *"The Government of the United States of America is not, in any sense, founded on the Christian religion."* April 19, 1803 brought yet another great insight of our Founding Fathers, when Thomas

Jefferson wrote to Edward Dowse and commented *"I never will, by any word or act, bow to the shrine of intolerance, or admit a right of inquiry into the religious opinions of others."* Jefferson also called for a 'wall of separation' between church and state.

Our very own U.S. Constitution, the Supreme Law of our land, addresses this same matter in the very amendment that gives you and me the freedom of speech. Even before that is mentioned, the First Amendment begins this way: *"Congress shall make no law respecting an establishment of religion, or prohibiting the free exercise thereof."* So tell me again why this was meant to be a Christian nation.

If someone should accept his or her country's culture, why didn't the early Christians accept the fact that this country had no state-regulated religion? Our nation was founded in 1776, yet "In God We Trust" did not appear on U.S. coins until 1908 and didn't make it to paper money until 1957. The Pledge of Allegiance was written in 1892 and survived a full 62 years without religion, until 1954, when *"under God"* was added due to protests by the Knights of Columbus, a Catholic organization. I agree that people should accept the culture of the country they live in, but the Christians of this nation sure haven't! They have completely taken over, even though our Constitution blatantly states no religion should be established.

By making the statement that this is a Christian Nation, American Christians are not only showing their lack of knowledge of our actual history, but alienating the Atheists, Agnostics, Muslims, Buddhists, Polytheists, Native Americans, and many other hard-working, tax-paying citizens who call this nation home and make our country a great place to live. Society has been trying for thousands of years to live in the presence of gods and has not yet found peace. In fact, it has resulted in millions of deaths and religious wars. So perhaps living *without* religion is the way to go.

Would our ethics remain solid without religion? We'd no longer have to live by ancient rules that barely make sense today. We could be genuinely happy and spend 10% of our money on homeless shelters and helping those in need, instead of paying our preacher's Cadillac payment. In gods we have *never* trusted. In each other, we have. But is this the way to live? Could we really make it as a society with this mind-set? My research continued.

# THE STOLEN HOLIDAY

As I examined and rejected the Christian faith, some aspects of the religious system tried to pull me back in, and at times, were quite convincing in doing so. I often wondered *"Why would so many people celebrate Christmas if Jesus wasn't something special?"* My first goal in answering this was to investigate the origins of Christmas to see where it really started, and what I discovered was monumental.

The key to success for any organization is being able to evolve and adapt to its society. If Christianity never changed from its original system, it wouldn't be around today. Like any major corporation, it learned to develop new ideas, and adopt popular cultures. Centuries before Jesus was ever said to live, people were celebrating births and life during the long dark days of winter. The holiday began in Northern Europe as what was called *Yule* at the time of the Winter Solstice, or the first day of winter. Families would bring evergreen trees indoors as reminders of life.

Ancient Romans celebrated *Saturnalia* just one week before the Winter Solstice, to commemorate Saturn the god of agriculture. Many Roman government officials believed that December 25th was the holiest day of the year, because it was the birthday of Mithras the sun god. It became a celebratory day called *Dies Natalis Soli Invicti"* which directly translates as '*The birthday of the unconquered Sun.*' It was reassuring to everyone that although it was getting colder, and the days were becoming shorter, the sun (and Mithras) would remain strong for all to live. This was a very powerful holiday, and with good reason. Approximately 100–200 years after Jesus was said to have died, Christianity began to take hold, but the birthday of Jesus was unknown. Since the winter holy day was already popular, the Christian Church simply designated December 25th as the birth of Christ and adopted the pagan traditions of bringing trees indoors. They essentially 'stole' the holiday from Mithras.

The *"reason for the season"* is actually to celebrate life, strength, and future, which is why I participate, and celebrate the Winter Solstice, as it was originally intended. It astonished me at first to discover that Jesus was not born on December 25th, and it only made me wonder, *"Was Jesus ever really born at all?"* The Bible scholars who do support the existence of Jesus claim that if he *was* born, it was probably around April.

The clearly erroneous notion that a person named Jesus Christ was born on December 25th had spread all over before our country was founded, and very few people knew the real history behind it. The churches were intentionally deceiving people to gain membership. They would not teach children of the other alleged gods that were said to be born on this date (Horus, Krishna, Mithras, among others, all share Dec. 25th). This discovery was the first time I actually felt deceived by Christianity and realized I'd been had. I immediately lost trust for Christian doctrine and realized it had been dishonest for over a thousand years. I could not put my faith into such an organization. Even though I considered myself Atheist at this point, I couldn't just shrug these things off as nonsense. So many people believed that Jesus was born on December 25th. I couldn't just let it go. Only a few minutes of research for me proved that to be false, yet millions take that, and parts of the Bible literally. I continued to search for answers for why so many people could blindly follow Christianity without asking more questions.

# PRAYER

As a young thinker, it raised an obvious red flag for me when I discovered that prayer was not allowed in schools. Obviously, someone very high up had the same concerns I did, and I needed to figure out why. If the existence of the Christian god was an absolute fact, why shouldn't the Christian message be spread everywhere? There was a disagreement somewhere, and I wanted to track that down. Even now, one of the most commonly debated topics of our time is the locations in which religious people can pray or state their message. I'm all for free speech, but could I scream on your porch? At what point do sidewalk preachers become abusive to their right of free speech? Should they be able to preach loudly in front of elementary schools during recess, with a captive audience of children? Where do we draw the line, and how can public prayer be a bad thing? These were more of the questions I asked along my journey.

Do you think we should have prayer in public schools? As you think of that question, you are probably imagining a wonderful school which allows not only a rich learning environment, but also one that provides an avenue of spirituality and the options for your children to stop and pray or openly discuss religion to have a closer relationship with their god. If that's your idea behind prayer in schools, your answer is probably "yes." Now, let's go through a couple of scenarios which may change your mind. Remember, our perception is our own personal reality.

(1) Your five-year-old daughter comes home from Kindergarten very excited, telling you all about how she got to stoop to her

knees in class, bow on a rug, and point towards something called the Mecca as she gave "praise to Allah," because other kids were doing it, and she thought it was "cool." Would you be okay with that?

(2) Your teenage Baptist son and daughter are placed in a class with a male Catholic teacher who tells them both that the use of condoms and birth control are interfering with his god's will and are therefore evil. He prays out-loud in front of the class that your family will one day find the 'truth' of the Catholic Church. Would you be okay with that?

These are just a couple of scenarios that could take your ultimate fantasy of education and worship and turn them into a nightmare. Prayer in public schools will simply lead to disaster, because the truth is, you will only support it as long as your child prays and worships the way *you* would. The reality is they will be exposed to so much more than you are willing to handle, and they will be subjected to an influential authority figure who may disagree with your beliefs. The structure of prayer would ultimately be influenced by the denomination of the teacher. Furthermore, you would run the risk of teachers playing favorites with children of the same belief system and mistreating those of different ones. I could only imagine my son, professing Atheism, and refusing to pray, and how he would be treated in a Texas elementary classroom! It's simply too much for the school to handle or maintain, and too much pressure to place on the children.

Our public schools are paid for with the tax dollars of Atheists, Agnostics, Hindus, Protestants, Methodists, Baptists, Muslims, Mormons, Jews, and just about every other denomination you can list. Through my personal discovery, I found that we should keep prayer in the religious buildings, and keep secular education separate. We can't teach the science of gravity and the story of a talking donkey in the same building! (See Numbers 22 in the Bible.) However, for many years, children of all religions were forced to follow along with prayers and other religious instructions led by teachers, whether the families liked it or not. Keep in mind; these were not private schools, but public, tax-supported schools.

What amazes me the most is that when someone finally spoke up for the rights of these children and families, and had 'forced prayer' removed from public schools, she was deemed by *Life* magazine to be *"the most hated woman in America."* Madalyn Murray O'Hair was only protecting the rights of school children all across the country so they could *choose* their religion and not have it forced upon them. Yet, because she was an Atheist activist, she was the enemy. Sadly, she was murdered in 1995, along with her son and granddaughter. Incredibly, many religious people have actually benefited from her activism as well. Catholic children in public schools aren't forced to recite Baptist prayers, and *vice-versa*. It is truly an honor to have my first book published by the organization she founded.

Many Christians, after I've asked enough difficult questions, will ultimately say that they just *know* their god is real because they *feel* him. They claim to have had personal experiences that have proven the Christian god's existence. I understand this notion, as I've often felt similar feelings. However, upon closer examination, these feelings and circumstances always have another, better explanation.

Perhaps you've found yourself in a hard financial situation and prayed about it. Amazingly, money arrived in the mail that you weren't expecting, and you honestly believe in your heart that 'God' took care of you. Because I can't prove that it did not come from Yahweh, the only thing left for me to do is ascertain if it's possible for this to happen without prayer.

Well, I am living, breathing proof that it is. Many years ago, I was personally experiencing a horrible financial strain, because one of our vehicles was totaled, and there as a problem with the insurance papers that prevented the insurance company from paying for it. My wife and I were stuck and we had no idea what to do. To top it off, we had just purchased a new home, and had plenty of moving expenses to take care of.

In an effort to test religion and prove a point using my own family as an example, we intentionally did *not* pray about our situation, or let any family members know what was going on. Without a single prayer, fast, sacrifice, or any other metaphysical or spiritual action on our side, we received a large check in the mail that was completely unexpected. It wasn't a gift but a totally unrelated technicality that forced a company to send us the check.

We were amazed and felt incredibly lucky. That money really helped us get through a slump. We also laughed and said that Christians would have considered that to be undeniable proof that prayer works, because we *know* they would have prayed every day through a situation like that. The Christian apologists that I've mentioned this to all said that me receiving the check just shows the awesome power and grace of their god to bless a household that didn't pray. The question is, if rewards come *without* prayer, and the will of the Christian god will be done *regardless*, why pray at all? It's so easy to make claims that can't be proven otherwise, and since it's impossible to prove a negative, I can't win that argument. I can only say that I know it's possible for things like that to happen without praying for it. Besides, if a Christian had prayed for that money, and received it, they couldn't prove that Satan didn't send that money just to tempt them! The burden of proving a negative goes both ways.

In July 2004, my father had a horrible accident that landed him in an ICU at a Dallas hospital. He was completely unconscious for nearly a month, and I was ultimately responsible for everything the doctors were doing. I had to give authorization for specific life-threatening surgeries and work with other family members, mostly his sister, to make arrangements for taking care of his personal life. I visited him almost daily and stayed in touch with the hospital staff. I spent my time doing research on his condition and the procedures they wanted to do so that I could make sound decisions. I never once prayed for the strength to get through it, or prayed for the knowledge to make good decisions, or even prayed for his recovery. I simply didn't think about it. I was just focused on making the best decisions possible, and trusting the doctors to do everything they could and made myself available. I'm happy to say he made a full recovery and returned to living a productive life. Again, Christians would have been praying the entire time for his recovery, and for help making those decisions, and would have attributed his success to their religion. Granted, I do not know if other family members prayed, but I know I didn't, and I know I had no help in making the decisions I made for him.

The thing about prayer is, *it can't be measured*, at least not to satisfy those who believe in it. Even if we *were* to test the results of prayer (which has been done) the response from apologists would simply depend on the results. If the test happened to conclude that prayer seemed to work, Christian apologists would simply use that to scientifically confirm their belief. If the results did *not* point to prayer working, they would say that their god somehow knew we were testing him, and chose not to participate. So there's always a safety net for the Christian apologists to fall back on.

When I approach them with stories like this, they say *"Just because you weren't praying for your father, it doesn't mean someone else wasn't praying for him."* There's nothing really to say to that. There is no proof that others weren't praying, and there is no proof that Yahweh didn't bless my home. But there also isn't proof that an invisible pink unicorn doesn't live in my closet. But you must ask yourself, *"How far am I willing to accept those beliefs without sufficient proof?"* especially now that you know amazing things happen to secular families that never pray at all.

People go to great lengths to show their devotion to gods. This is probably the most sensitive chapter in this book and by far the most difficult to write. Let me begin by stating the last thing I would ever want to do is judge someone in a critical situation or criticize someone for doing the best they can for their loved ones in dire needs. However, some of the actions of the following people have shocked the world, and for better or worse, it was all done in the name of the Christian god.

A mother in California learned that her young child was diagnosed with cancer. As this would be sad news to anyone, many people rushed to her aid offering different types of treatment. The mother publicly refused all medical treatment for her child. She stated that Jesus would save him and chose to only 'treat' the child with prayer. She refused multiple chemotherapy treatments. Sadly, the child died. Regardless of her motive or belief, the California Supreme Court ruled that her actions resulted in the death of a child and therefore convicted her of involuntary manslaughter and child endangerment. It's a bit ironic that behind the Justice's bench making the ruling are plastered the words "IN GOD WE TRUST," yet they are convicting her for doing just that!

According to Christian apologists, she should have included 'works' with her prayer, which would include allowing the doctors to perform their duties in an effort to save the child. This is an understandable argument. However, the final comments of Christian apologists in her defense were *"God wanted the boy to come home and be with him in Heaven, and it was just his time to go."* So ultimately, Christians believe that regardless of how you treat an illness, if Yahweh is ready for you to 'come home,' you will die. If that's the case, the woman was right in her actions. After all, in her opinion, she only let her god's will be done. This is when things become very serious, and religious beliefs become very dangerous.

Another surprising example of prayer abuse is when the champion fighter catches his opponent with a right hook, busting his nose open. With blood flying, causing him to drop to the mat unconscious, doctors rush into the ring to make an attempt to revive the downed man. Meanwhile, the champion cheers for his victory. In the post fight interview, when asked why the fight went his way, the champion states *"You can do anything with God on your side. I just prayed about it, and God granted me the strength to come out the winner in this one."* Are you kidding me? Does that statement not greatly offend Christians all over the world? How arrogant must you be to think that a righteous and holy god would give you the strength to beat someone to an unconscious state for the purpose of sport? What if both fighters prayed before the fight? What about when Atheists, Muslims, or other denominations within Christianity win the fight over a Baptist? This notion is quite absurd.

Many times you hear on the news of a child being kidnapped. As the time passes, the probability of the child returning dwindles. Yet miraculously, some children are returned after weeks or even months of absence. The first thing out of the parent's mouth is always, *"We knew God would bring her home."* This really bothers me. What about all the people who prayed for their children, only to have the bodies found in a ditch? Should they now believe the Christian god doesn't love their child as much? Perhaps they can believe that the Christian god in fact loved their child more, therefore demanded she come to Heaven immediately, because he was "missing an angel." Whatever these families believe to make themselves feel better is fine with me. But coming out and saying that a god had a direct hand in it really begins to pit people against one another in the fight for the Christian god's love and attention. Is this what religion was designed for? Is this the miracle of prayer at work?

The unfortunate thing is, sometimes, a person prays and receives the desired result. This is the most dangerous. To a skeptic, the result is nothing more than a coincidence or the most possible circumstantial solution. To a Christian, it happened because they prayed. This results in the beliefs and expectation of prayer, which often times results in overlooked responsibility and disappointment. The passive nature that comes with Christianity has directly resulted in a person to give up when things become difficult. Regardless of your religious beliefs, you must agree to take responsibility for your actions, and understand that you should do everything in your power to prevent harm or unjust actions or poverty that may strike your family. Do not let Jesus take your wheel. Drive to your own destiny until your wheels fall off.

Despite my thoughts on prayer, I do not place it in a category of 'uselessness' as you may think. Many religious people utilize prayer as 'evil prevention,' and believe it or not, I actually feel this can work. As people talk through things out loud (as they think they are talking to their god), it can be very therapeutic and have positive psychological effects. Children can remove bad dreams, prevent bed wetting, and calm themselves from anxiety by believing in their hearts that a god is taking care of the problem, when in reality, they are training their psyche to remove a problem that never really existed to begin with. Effectively, prayer can be credited with the absence of ghosts, just as leprechauns can be credited with the absence of unicorns. In most cases, this brings no harm. However, when people of power, such as politicians, begin to rely on the leprechauns for success and protection, or as George W. Bush did, by making his god part of his foreign policy, it becomes a real danger to society.

The issue I take with this is that Christians actually pray to prevent something, which according to their belief, shouldn't exist by definition. As I have probed many Christians before on the topic of evil, the average apologist will say that evil was not created by 'God,' it is the absence of the deity. While that sounds very good during a debate, and will get a cheer from the Christian crowd, we must remind them of their other description of *God*. By definition, he is said to be omnipresent (everywhere, all the time). Therefore, as I previously mentioned, how could we ever be "without him?"

If bad things happening are proof that a particular god is not present in those places, yet that god is supposed to be everywhere, all the time, then each bad thing that happens is therefore proof that the Christian god is either imaginary, or otherwise quite absent from many things, of which he is *supposed* to be involved. Furthermore, as I briefly mentioned earlier in the chapter, Yahweh is said to be all things good and all things powerful, and everywhere, until of course it is convenient for Christians for him to have human limitations, such as not being allowed in schools, or being removed from our courtrooms.

During religious debates, as I began to reject spiritual theories altogether, I was often challenged to explain the presence of evil. Christians would ask, *"How could there be such harsh acts, wrong-doing and bad people if pure evil does not exist in spiritual form?"*

In addressing this challenge, we must concede that the word *evil* has subjective definitions equating it to 'bad' or 'wrong'; therefore, the word itself cannot be discarded altogether. In an effort to accurately convey our message, we must address this conceptually by asserting that we are only referring to the 'spiritual' use of the word, as in "Where does the spirit of evil come from, and how does it exist?" Effectively, we are debating why bad things happen.

When presented with such a question, at first blush, it appears to be a powerful debate technique used by one's opponent, in which the believer attempts to lead the nonbeliever into speaking religious language. We are surely expected to respond with something about 'Satan' or 'demons,' or perhaps answering with the obvious 'opposite of good' theory, at which point we are trapped into defining good and its source. As American Atheist Press author David Eller warns in his book *Atheism Advanced*, we must be careful not to "speak Christian" and only debate in terms which are meaningful. There is a difference between a word having a definition and having a true meaning. The book's example points to unicorns. We all know the definition and can picture one, but what meaning does it really have? There is no real substance or truth to a unicorn; therefore it is a meaningless term with a definition (Eller 2007). We can apply that frame of thought to the word 'evil.' While we can all recite a basic definition of the word, no one could ever define its true meaning, or provide a real source. It is hardly a meaningful term in the spiritual sense. We can only assume it derives from a lower or bad god, and begin to project our opinions. When believers profess that evil is the opposite of good, we should ask them to give good a meaning, not just a definition. It may seem like semantics, but isn't that really what religion is built on anyway?

Pointing back to Dr. David Eller, his recent book also mentions a psychologist by the name of Roy Baumeister, the author of *Evil: Inside Human Violence and Cruelty* (2001). He finds that people tend to blame their own negative behavior on external sources, stating that they are relatively good people in bad situations. When surveyed, these same people attribute the negative acts of others to evil, blaming their deviant personalities (Eller 2007). This study only furthers the notion that spiritual evil and pure evil are simply fictitious excuses for negative behavior without accountability.

Regardless of the semantics involved, or studies we have done, believers will often resort to their own experiences, citing an 'evil feeling' at a point when they lost control. This in fact does happen but has nothing to do with evil spirits.

In studying cognitive psychology, we learn that when a person reaches a level of stress, especially in the forms of fear or anger, blood flow to the brain is actually restricted, thereby reducing the ability to think clearly. The body is then pumped with adrenalin and cortisol, which must be expressed in some way. Some people cry (expressing most of the cortisol in the release of tears), others express adrenalin with anger and violence, and some of us do both. There is no doubt that persons under the influence of their own stress will make poor decisions, act violently, and perhaps even describe the experience as 'out of body,' because they didn't have full control; but *evil* has nothing to do with it. This further perpetuates the long running fallacy of believers explaining that which they do not understand as spiritual or metaphysical.

So what are child molesters and rapists? What was Hitler, if not evil? There is no doubt that bad things and bad people exist in the world. However, they do so for many reasons other than pure evil inside them. Personal choices, genetics, greed, wrongful motivation, and misinterpretations all contribute to a person's negative actions. In fact, in a speech, Hitler said *"I believe today that I am acting in the sense of the Almighty Creator. By warding off the Jews I am fighting for the Lord's work."* It is evident, that in Hitler's mind, the Jews were evil. And Hitler was not the first person to assert that—and to act on it! But was Hitler evil? Or did he simply misinterpret religious doctrine and become wrongly motivated to commit mass murder? Perhaps he developed mental disturbances that caused his actions; but *spiritually* evil? In order to claim that, we would have to obtain an objective meaning of the word, and again, that appears impossible due to its meaningless status.

Early humans blamed evil for hurricanes, floods, and other natural disasters. Now, we understand the meteorology behind the storms and can confidently state an evil spirit is not sending storms as torture for mankind. In the study of law, we find that humans have blamed evil forces for their wrong-doing since crime was recorded. In criminology, the psychological study of the criminal mind, we find the statement *"Where gods reign, demons exist as well"* (Winfree & Abadinsky 2003). According to the same authors, in *Understanding Crime, Theory and Practice*, a further correlation was made by the early psychologist Dr. William Sheldon, who noted that during the phases of embryonic development, a human baby begins to take a specific physical form. Once a particular body type dominates, it is called the somatotype. Upon studying 200 young criminals and comparing them to 200 college students, a specific difference was noticed by the doctor. A majority of the criminals belonged to the same somatotype, which differed from the students' (Sheldon, 1949). This suggests that 'evil' in humans is not a spirit at all, but perhaps an inherent deformity during embryonic growth that is invisible to the naked eye.

To further add to the impossibilities of evil spirits or pure evil, we ask the question, "Why are good people good?" Let me remind the readers of the secular humanists' work to help the homeless, volunteer, and reach out to those in need. Hundreds of thousands of secular humanists across the world have a strong sense of family pride and strive daily to succeed both materially and ethically. If a god is said to be responsible for the good in the hearts of secular humanists, why did it not place the fundamentals of belief there as well? We ethical nonbelievers are living proof that a person can have good will without a god's will.

Condensing the theory of evil down to five parts, we see that (1) A person does not need a good 'spiritual source' to be good; (2) People can perform evil acts when they think they are doing good ones; (3) A person can exhibit evil traits due to developmental bias; and (4) There has been no source proven as an absolute necessity for either good or evil. This only leaves one final statement: (5) An 'evil spirit' is not necessary for negative acts to be performed.

As we now see, multiple things can lead to the appearance of evil, yet 'evil' has never truly appeared. In the words of Delo McKown, *"The invisible and the non-existent look very much alike. "* Evil is no more existent in the absolute form, than good, gods, or unicorns! Moreover, that makes prayer against evil futile; unless of course the verbal therapy helps you cope.

It was once said that a thousand heads bowed in prayer are greater than a single good deed done by a single good heart. Atheists blatantly disagree with this statement, promoting care and love for your fellow man rather than praying to a god. In any event, since Christians do believe prayer is better than good deeds, where is the line drawn? There must be a line of progression, with a stopping point, to where action supersedes prayer. So let's go through a few scenarios and think about where your beliefs lead you:

- You and I are both walking in the city. We see an elderly lady slowly struggling to cross the street. You are running late on your way to church and pass her by so that you can go pray. I go out of my way to ensure her safety and assist her. Which is better: helping my fellow mankind, or your prayer and worship?

- Your church is suffering financially and is just about to be closed. Would you rather me give you $20,000 to save the church, or for all the church members to bow their heads and pray to the Christian god for strength to provide a solution?

- You are driving to church in the pouring rain. You almost make it there, and you see a dear friend, who happens to be an Atheist, walking. He is soaking wet from the rain and looks miserable. Taking him to church with you is not an option. If you stop to pick him up, you will have to take him home and be forced to miss church services for the day. What do you do? Is it better to pass him by, get to church, and pray for his safe return home? Or is the single good deed to help your fellow man better than prayer in this case?

Regardless of how you would personally react in these situations, two things are clear: we know that good things happen without prayer; and even with prayers to prevent them, bad things happen as well, seemingly at the same statistical rates to everyone. So I may not be able to prove that prayer doesn't help, but I've certainly proved that it's not necessary, and has little to no correlation with things *actually* happening.

## CHILD LABOR IN RELIGION

In December 2008, the *Christian Post* Web-site openly announced the use of child labor to evangelize for Christ in an effort to recruit other children online. The organizer of the "online missions" said this was a *"two-week opportunity for all of us to bombard Facebook, MySpace, YouTube, Twitter, whatever social places you go to online, with the Gospel of Jesus Christ."*

I sent a letter to the organizer, Tim, as follows:

*Tim,*

*I honestly think it's disturbing that you are encouraging these churches to use vulnerable children to push their message of religiosity to other children. A child cannot make the distinction between reason and reality, let alone teach it to others. These children have not had the opportunity to learn about Secular Humanism, Buddhism, Islam, Hinduism, or any other religion. These children are not Christians—they are the offspring of Christian parents and nothing more in the religious sense. They do not have the capacity to accept Christianity as truth. Having Christian parents does not qualify them to become evangelists for Christ, and requesting them to do so is brainwashing, mental child abuse, and forcible child labor for your private cause.*

*Tim, why don't you give these children the opportunity to grow up on their own, and instead of scaring them with the notions of*

*Hell and prompting them to make fearful decisions, encourage them to make educated ones? Before they go on your mission, that they don't fully understand, let them read 'The God Delusion' by Richard Dawkins, or 'Atheism Advanced' by Dr. David Eller which completely deconstructs all religions piece by piece. Even let them read my blog! Then, when they have obtained equal knowledge on the topics of religion you have pushed on them, let them compare that to the logic of the Holy Bible where we see a talking snake and donkey.*

*This use of child labor is an outrage. Please use only willing adults to push your religious message.*

*—David Smalley*

This is a reason why Atheists become activists. Tim responded by claiming that these children had given their consent, and "most of them" were at least sixteen to seventeen years old and were not forced at all. He also suggested that I must have a minimal knowledge of religion and shouldn't be taken seriously. I don't doubt that the children agreed to participate, but how could they possibly understand what they were agreeing to?

My reply:

*Tim,*

*Please tell me why these same sixteen-year-olds cannot enter into a legal agreement. Why can't they buy a car, sign a lease, purchase alcohol, use tobacco, become wed, enter the military, or otherwise act independently in a social structure?*

*It's because it is widely accepted that teenagers do not yet have the capacity to fully understand what they are getting themselves into. It is obvious that this is not unlawful 'child labor' in the legal sense, but you are coercing young minds that have been influenced from your teachings starting at an early age, and utilizing that coercion to create immature robot evangelizers to spread your popular cult's message on the Web.*

*Then, what happens when teens in your area reach out to other teens, and they show up to your church? More tithes! That's what happens. You will be financially gaining from the works and labors of children in the name of the Christian god, by coercing them to 'bombard' secular Web-sites. Would you not be disturbed if you witnessed sixteen-year-old children of Wicca parents knocking on doors, informing the general public of the uses of goat's blood? Surely that would bother you, just the same as this bothers me. You are creating an army of mentally immature web-soldiers to spread a message they don't fully understand.*

*Have you taught these kids about Genesis 22 and had them think of what it must have been like to be Isaac? Do they understand how wrathful the supposed god appears to be in the religious doctrine you support as fact? Do these kids know about Mithras and the familiar similarities of where Christianity stole its basis? Have they been taught of the Winter Solstice, and pagan traditions that began what you now call 'Christmas?' No, they have only been taught your biased view on Christianity, and told that if they do not follow, they will burn in Hell. That sickens me.*

*As for my knowledge of religion, it is often said that an Atheist is not one who knows too little about religion, but one who knows too much. I know your canned, scripted responses before you think them. I know your Bible better than you, because I have proven most of it to be full of fallacies. It is you and your group who need the education. Please, just stop using children to further your agenda. You are only hurting your own religion's reputation.*

*As for your claim of the children's ages, I will not be convinced for one moment that only sixteen and seventeen-year-olds are participating. We all know that younger children are taking part, but you won't admit that in this reply to me.*

*Regardless, the meaningful purpose of the age eighteen will forever be debatable, but the point is not the specific age of accountability. It is the conceptual view that our society separates children from adults for specific reasons. Children lack certain capacities, and we adults frown upon others that take advantage of those shortcomings. You and your group are attempting to capitalize on using children for your own agenda, and the children do not know enough to refute the claims.*

*Again, these are the same reasons police do not typically question sixteen-year-olds after crimes unless an attorney is present, because they know how a child's promise could be altered by a powerful adult figure, and said testimony, even a confession, would likely be thrown out. The same goes here. You mentioned in your reply to me, that these children are not being used, but that this is "totally an optional act of their free will." Your co-worker then came to my blog, and stated that this was an opportunity for those wanting to "take the next step in their relationship with*

*God." Don't you see what's happening here? No, these children are not being physically forced to work in a sweat shop, but do they really have a choice under such circumstances? Is that your definition of 'free will?'*

*Christianity teaches that if you refuse their god, you will burn in Hell. Furthermore, Matthew 7:21 states that knowing this god is not simply enough, but in order to enter the kingdom of Heaven, one must "doeth the will of my Father which is in Heaven."— (which I'm sure is a verse you frequently use in your brainwashing sessions)—so you tell me, does it sound like these children have a choice?*

—David Smalley

I often find myself defending the defenseless, yet I'm viewed in the public eye as enemy number one, simply for not believing. I just hope that one day people will understand what they're doing to the children of our society. Perhaps all I can do is save my own.

# INDUCED PSYCHOSIS:

# THE INVISIBLE CHILD ABUSE

As a larger part of my quest for helping people in need, namely the homeless, and gathering information about why most people believe in religions, I began studying psychology. Throughout my studies, I've learned about many issues in child development, ranging from language disorders, to drug and alcohol abuse, and everything in between. Many psychologists have studied the effects of parenting styles, environment, and culture, and how they relate to specific developmental disorders in children.

It is regularly overlooked due to a falsely obtained positive reputation, but instilling religion and structured spiritual beliefs into children may very well create an entirely new set of sociological and developmental problems. Psychosis is a psychiatric disorder that is marked by delusions, hallucinations, incoherence, and distorted perceptions of reality, and we should really take a close look into what religion brings to our families.

Making children believe there are things watching them at all times, that evil and demons exist in unstoppable spiritual form, or that they themselves are inherently evil and must fight their instincts, is really a form of child abuse when you break it down to what it causes in the long term.

From the stages of infancy, all children are drawn to images like their own and seek protection in larger more powerful versions of themselves. This is, in part, where the concept of gods derived coupled with memories of dead loved ones and feelings, which are ignited when those memories are retrieved (Eller 2007). We naturally have the desire to gravitate towards more powerful versions of our self, which is why Albert Einstein said, *"human fantasy made God in man's own image."* (That's right, Albert Einstein did not believe in any personal god.)

Even the newborns of various animal species know to stick together for protection and remain close to other animals they can relate to, yet they are not said to have spirits or souls in the Christian belief. Unfortunately for our society, most human adults do not lose this natural need. As adolescents become adults, they do not want to be held responsible for everything that happens, nor do they want the responsibility of everyone's safety. Therefore, it is somewhat of a natural progression for grown men and women to create something more powerful than themselves on which to place the liability of human kind. This has resulted in the creation of gods and spirits that people claim are watching over them for protection and amazingly look somewhat human when drawn or described. It is said that the Christian god made man in his own image, but perhaps it's the other way around, and millions of Christian parents are in fact inducing a form of psychosis in their offspring. This explains (at least in part) why religions continue to thrive.

The journey of the Christian child begins when he or she is taught at just three years old to repeat specific chants and songs in Sunday school. One specific Christian chant begins with this verse: *"Jesus loves me, this I know, for the Bible tells me so. Little ones to him belong; they are weak but he is strong."* There are subliminal messages in this chant, which create the beginnings of brainwashing and low self-esteem.

First of all, the Bible is immediately shown as the absolute source of knowledge and fact because it 'proves' that Jesus loves the singing child. This presents the book as infallible, which is misleading to say the least. Many adults grow up referring to the Bible as ultimate fact, and any evidence proving otherwise creates friction, regardless of how scientifically correct it may be. Furthermore, the singing child is taught that they are weak, and Jesus is strong. This instantly puts the child in a submissive, follower role instead of building the child's confidence to be a leader and freethinker. This is the beginning of the mental abuse.

Inducement of psychosis continues as the child attends religious private schools or consistent Bible studies that teach mythical stories as historical fact. The first problem here is that many of the stories strictly contradict science and reasonable thought, such as a talking serpent (Genesis 3:4), a talking donkey (Numbers 22:28), or a scientifically impossible feat of paired creatures and a meteorologically impossible flood (Genesis 7).

This not only places false information into the child's memory but also drastically affects the way one reasons and makes decisions, distinguishing fact from fantasy in the future. This makes it very difficult for the child to process future lessons he or she may learn about biology and chemical compounds of salt water versus fresh water, which was eloquently pointed out by Frank Zindler in the television debate mentioned above (*transcript available at atheists.org*). This causes the child to enter society with a religious bias, because they have already learned about things in a spiritual format, so naturally, any secular scientific information which may contradict their prior lessons will be viewed as *false*, *heresy*, or *anit-God*.

This is not giving the children a fair chance with their lives, or a head start, but is instead creating obstacles for future education and the potential of learning disabilities and confusion of what type of material to trust. Many of these children grow up missing basic historical facts, such as the history of the Winter Solstice, along with pagan traditions adopted by Christians due to popularity. Sociological pressure also plays a role as the children enter adolescence, and they begin to hear the word 'Christian' replace the word 'good' when describing a family member, a neighbor, or a baby sitter. This subliminal secret often makes non-Christians want to hide their belief status, because simple logic tells us if 'Christian' equals 'good,' then anything else (especially that which opposes Christianity) is obviously less than favorable, and an embarrassment.

Adolescents wishing to avoid these negative labels claim to be Christian and follow church practices in an attempt to become, or at least appear, Christian. These religiously biased views also pour over into how the child judges others, even by the small sample of actions they have seen in their own group (Klaczynski, 2000).

It's quite possible that teen depression could also stem from religious teachings, in that children are taught that they are inherently evil and should essentially repent and apologize for being born. This is an awful notion to place in someone's mind and can obviously become detrimental to self-esteem, self-confidence, and one's ability to succeed while being constantly instructed to *"place it in God's hands"* or *"let go and let God."*

The inducement of psychosis doesn't stop with teenagers. I had the pleasure of being heard on KLIF Talk Radio on 570 AM in Dallas (a Fox affiliate). The conservative morning-show host,

Jeff Bolton, began the conservation by saying: *"I agree that our government shouldn't endorse a particular religion, but anyone that says 'God' should be removed from our money is a moron and shouldn't be heard."*

My immediate response corrected the stereotype, when I told him it was *"completely inappropriate to call someone a moron for simply disagreeing."* Then, I confirmed my purpose with a question: *"Jeff, when our government allowed the word 'God' to appear on our money, whom were they referring to?"*

It's not common for a talk show host to be silenced, but since he didn't answer, I continued... "Poseidon? Mithra? Zeus?" Still with no answer, I decided to remove the awkwardness. *"Everyone can agree they were referring to Yahweh, the god of Christianity. Now tell me how that's not endorsing a particular belief system."*

I then elaborated on the many years our government lasted without religion by proving that our Pledge of Allegiance was written in 1892, but the words "under God" weren't added until 62 years later, after protests by the Knights of Columbus (a Catholic organization). In this way, our government has influenced our children to lean towards Christianity by having them recite an allegiance to a nation under a *specific* god and having them spend money that references that same *specific* god. The government is very influential and is a trusted source for young people as an authority figure; and they too are helping to induce psychosis and continue the disorder throughout adulthood.

Starting a child off on a journey of spiritual and religious beliefs filled with guilt, repentance, and remorse cannot be good for one's ethical development. Despite the many goods that come from some religions, so much psychosis is spawned from it; it shouldn't be seen as an overall positive style of parenting. It is truly harmful to the core and creates its own developmental issues that are rarely addressed. As I attempt to defend children from this mental abuse, I am looked upon as the "Anti-Christ" stopping children from finding their savior, when in fact, that's exactly what I'm trying to do—save them.

## PREJUDICE AND BLIND ACCEPTANCE

The discoveries of these horrible sides of Christianity that our preachers never taught us led me to question why people actually do follow this collection of religions. How can it sustain such a large following and keep such a positive reputation of being the right thing to do when it clearly portrays attributes of being the worst possible decision one could make?

One of the main things that sparked my deep interest in religion—and began my education in psychology—is how otherwise intelligent people, who use reason and logic on a daily basis, can completely abandon that problem-solving heuristic to accept a religion as truth without fundamental proof. We're talking about successful people in the world—CEO's, senators, doctors, and even scientists who believe in a talking snake. I'm amazed that they can go about their normal day, using typical problem solving skills and reason, and then go home, read the Bible, and actually believe that we live in a world where there is a virtual battle of good versus evil being fought using humans in a struggle over control of the universe. It sounds like such a Sci-Fi movie plot to me, but for many successful people, it is very real. Could they all be wrong? Should I just accept it because successful people believe it? Well, after thirteen years of researching it for myself, I have finally concluded exactly how that happens, from a psychological perspective.

Our ability to make logical decisions based on reason and value is what sets us apart from other creatures on this planet. However, we also have an amazing memory and adaptive ability of 'automaticity,' which allows us to learn tasks and become faster and better at them through an automatic cognitive process. This same function also helps us to relate stories and words with instant feelings without thinking. As an example, we're taught to just know that 4 x 4 = 16, Christian = good, Atheist = bad.

Over time, this can become detrimental to learning or accepting new definitions for certain words as we grow older and obtain further knowledge due to over-representation of fallacies. When we hear these words that had an initial negative impact on us and were overrepresented in our childhood, our long-term memory retrieves an instant feeling related to that event, and we immediately shun all reason or objective thinking that could otherwise be true. This cognitive process is referred to as bias encoding (Robinson-Riegler 2008).

An excellent demonstration of the ideology stated above would be the feeling you get when you hear that someone is an Atheist. Despite its literal meaning, which I've previously addressed and will delve into further in a moment, you have most likely related negative feelings to this word due to your bias encoding. In mid-2008, I was talking with a friend of mine who had been attending Catholic school for over 35 years and is well into his forties. He is still attending church to this day and considers himself a practicing Catholic. I asked him what being an 'Atheist' meant, and his response was *"It means you believe in the Devil, and not in God, and you sacrifice animals to Satan."* I was awed by his honesty, and amused at the same time, because he was serious. I couldn't help but laugh out loud at his ignorance of the word.

In fact, during one of my early child psychology classes, I mentioned that I was an Atheist, and my dear professor said, *"I'm just going to leave that alone—let's move on!"* I must wonder: if someone had said they were Protestant, or Baptist, would she have given the same reaction? The truth is an Atheist is just the opposite of a theist, who believes in a spiritual world or divine creator. An Atheist rejects all super-natural existence and prefers to live by empiricism, the theory that knowledge can be acquired only through direct observation and experimentation rather than through metaphysics and theology.

As I've previously stated, an Atheist is also typically referred to as a Secular Humanist, volunteering for local homeless shelters and reaching out to help humanity rather than worshipping a god. It's more about a redirection of resources away from religion and toward humanity. It's really that simple, but the bias encoding of a pseudo-religious society has made us believe that the godless is evil, and if you are not working for the Christian god, you are therefore against that god, and if you are an Atheist, you are the Anti-Christ. The irony of it is, many times, Atheists are saddled with 'Satanic rituals' when in fact, Atheists don't believe in any spirits or gods at all, including *bad* ones! Not to mention, the amount of animal and human sacrifices ordered in the Holy Bible by Yahweh is one of the main reasons many people reject Christianity and begin to consider Atheism in the first place! Freethinkers begin to read the awful stories in the biblical texts and wonder how one could worship a god that seems so maniacal.

The same stigma have been placed on words like *infidel* and *heathen*, as previously mentioned. Before picking up this book, you would have most likely seen those words and thought 'bad guy' and 'bratty child' respectively. These are not words to describe *bad people*, but have instead become *bad words* to describe *good people*. The sad part is, due to the sociological acceptance of these new virtual meanings, words like this are not considered offensive—simply because of which people they offend. In the public opinion, godless people are hardly considered people at all, and it's certainly okay to publicly make fun of them as President George H.W. Bush, did. Again, this goes back to the mind-set of societal grouping and making fun of anyone who doesn't believe the way we do. Society would like us to believe that Christians are good people and do things in a very Christian way that is respectable. But do they really? Would it ever be acceptable to stand up to a Christian and disagree with the mistreatment of others?

We can see that events stored in our long-term memory from childhood, such as being told we must go to church, and anyone who refuses to, is bad, wrong, and evil, have become encoded in us to immediately and automatically have negative feelings upon hearing certain words to describe these groups of people. If you disagree with Atheism, it should be the same as you disagreeing with Methodists or Mormons, not putting a fear of evil into you.

Now that I could categorize people and look into what the different beliefs actually meant, it was time to find out how people typically come to their decisions. Are there miracles happening that convert individuals, or are there cognitive psychological events taking place that explain these feelings?

As I continued to study the topic of Christianity, and religious individuals as a whole, I often ran into yet another cognitive process that is an enormous obstacle. I would often debate with Christians because I wanted to know their reasoning for choosing that system of beliefs. As I would present evidence of nearly ten thousand other religions to a Christian during a debate, to point out where religion itself came from, and explain how the thought of gods originated in mankind, I constantly hit a wall of what's known as *confirmatory bias*. This is the cognitive process in which only data that support the hypothesis are sought after (Robinson-Riegler, 2008). Individuals doing the research make up their mind of what the outcome should be prior to testing, and only search for evidence that proves them right, rejecting all evidence to the contrary. We should hardly call these people scientists, because they are more like the apologists I mentioned earlier, searching for ways to be right instead of looking for the most logical answer.

Christians point to the Bible as proof of Yahweh, so I pull up a biblical scripture that says, *"it is shameful for women to speak in church"* which can be found in 1 Timothy 2, and ask their opinion of that and request them to explain the sexist remark in their holy book. Their response is always something defensive or apologetic, and that times were different then. So my next response is, if the Bible had an omniscient and omnipresent source of inspiration, it would not be limited to the times, or to the knowledge of the authors who wrote it. Again, more apologetics come from them as they attempt to seek data that only show that their god exists and that their book is true, instead of stepping back and questioning their actions and beliefs. During my research, I often pondered why people would stop at nothing to defend their beliefs. The confirmatory bias cognitive process, and ingrained group-psychology discussed in the next session, are very good reasons why.

I can honestly say, as a Democrat, that I listen to conservative, Republican talk radio. As a skeptic, I listened to Christian and Catholic radio. I read the Bible and went to churches to learn and debate with preachers. I was truly fact-finding to determine why people believe the way they do, and I welcomed all knowledge, and still do. Most people who have accepted a particular religion refuse any and all data that could potentially prove that religion to be a fallacy and intentionally search for data that prove their hypothesis instead of reasonably questioning their actions and beliefs. But of course, that's what their religions instruct them to do, so it's really not surprising.

Confirmatory bias and bias encoding are the two most challenging cognitive processes I struggle to overcome in my opponents in religious debates. Furthermore, they are often caught up in the following method of problem solving. The basic principle is *"The Bible is the Word of God."* But how do we know? *"The Bible tells us so."* Why should we trust the Bible? *"The Bible is infallible."* What makes the Bible infallible? *"The Bible is the Word of God."* This is known as circular reasoning and does not lead to answers but only to more questions, followed by apologetics fueled with bias encoding.

As I present evidence contrary to any of the above circular reasoning statements, the confirmatory bias of theists has them searching for answers of validity in the very book I am asking them to validate. Simply put, you cannot convert an Atheist to

Christianity by citing the very doctrine he or she rejects. Proof must come from outside sources and be logical, reasonable, convincing, and obtained through empiricism. No religious doctrine in history has been proven as absolute; therefore none of them fit that description.

## GROUP PSYCHOLOGY

A friend of mine makes jokes that his father is so enthralled in a particular religion that he may one day watch a movie and then call the church to find out if he liked it! For the extremes, that becomes a very real possibility, and there is a logical reason. The religious man in question is no longer just a member of a group, but that group is now a member of him! Stay with me.

I was always convinced that the power and growth of religion were due to more than just a fear of eternal punishment, but I could never put my finger on it. Very few people would accept similar ideology if it were introduced as 'new' today, (*i.e.* the failure of David Koresh and Jim Jones). So why do we, as a 21st-century society, keep religious beliefs and traditions, other than because they are just, well... 'traditional'?

I have discovered my answer, and it sheds some light on why Christians feel so closely entwined with their theism and can't really explain why they have chosen that particular one. Most people (with the exception of a few preachers who are close friends of mine), when asked why they chose a particular denomination or specific god to worship, usually make mention of family traditions or respond with the more honest answer of, *"I'm not sure; I just know all the motions and songs, and this is the church my mom went to."* I'm sure even the preachers would agree this is not a valid reason to attend church.

Through my research, I've found a more logical explanation of religion's success, from a psychological approach. In reading on the history of psychology, and doing my public research on Atheism, I noticed some correlations famous psychologist Sigmund Freud made during his group psychology work and realized a similar topic was also covered in Dr. David Eller's book, *Atheism Advanced* (2007). I found that Freud's theory is an excellent explanation for why many people see religion as a social structure, and have a hard time breaking away, despite it making claims they may not agree with. It's not just about emotions, bonds, friendships, or even beliefs!

As with the religious folks in your family, the group as a whole becomes its own entity and therefore develops its own "group psychology" as Freud termed it, where people are almost in a trance-like or hypnotic state, performing group actions instead of individual ones (Freud, 1921). This isn't as mystical as it may sound. Many of us experience this on a regular basis. We laugh out loud while watching a funny movie with friends, when we might otherwise just enjoy it silently if we were alone. We also act differently at parties or other social settings and do things we wouldn't normally do in the company of just one friend, such as sing Karaoke or dancing. (The next time you have just one friend over, turn on some music and start dancing. Record their actions and email it to me. I'd love to have a good laugh!)

Religions aren't just social on the outside. Freud discovered that humans actually integrate themselves into groups by fundamentally replacing a piece of themselves with the attributes of a group, in whole or in part. With a more modern explanation, Eller writes, *"Within groups, negative attitudes toward other members are minimized or denied, resulting in narcissism toward the group and aversion or hostility toward outsiders; such groups tend to overlook the failings of their own"* (246). This is why people make excuses for their preacher not having all the answers!

Freud also observed that groups as a whole take on their own egos and mannerisms, and most times, the ego of the individual is actually *replaced* by the group's ego. This means that the group member will be willing to do things against his or her own ego or will, that he or she wouldn't normally do, simply because the individual's original ego is hardly existent when the group's ego is present.

To see your own example of this, watch *Family Feud* sometime. At the end of the round, when the remaining answers are shown to the studio audience, everyone reads them aloud together, very slowly, and collectively, so everyone can be on the same syllables. If a solitary person were shown that word privately, reading aloud would be at a normal speed, much faster than that of a crowd trying to stay together. In this example, the group takes on its own method of communication, as a separate entity from the individual; and there's nothing mystical about it.

Freud concluded his research with the saying, *"A panic arises if a group of that kind becomes disintegrated"* (Freud, 1921 p.35). This is because the member and the group have become integrated, and each is dependent upon the other to survive. Eller warns that this is why it is so difficult to *"de-convert a member of a church... it is then tearing out a piece of oneself"* (Eller, 2007 p.246).

This offers an explanation of why many Christians involuntarily and immediately reject any evidence not supporting their belief, even though they may subconsciously realize it does seem a little far-fetched. An accusation against your religion is now taken as a personal attack, because you are at one with your group, whether you realize it or not.

I have found that this doesn't just pertain to those who are part of a specific religion but also to theists generally. The common belief theism holds essentially creates a group-type mentality. It becomes its own socially charged religion, with opponents (that would be me) that (as Eller also warns) are necessary for any group to thrive.

I know what you're thinking. Don't Atheists join groups? Yes. But why does no atheistic organization have millions of members or reign as a dominant figure over governments as religions do? Either not enough Atheists join groups because they are solitary by nature, or a collective group of solitary thinkers does not make for a very powerful group; but the reality is that there will probably never be a powerhouse Atheist organization. The reason is simple. All groups at some point do form a group psychology. With Atheists being independent thinkers, they treasure their personal psychology and will not conform to that mentality. Atheists group—but not like theists.

We must be mindful of the effects that large groups can have on people and genuinely strive to be a collection of individual freethinkers as opposed to a collection of thoughts spewed by religious speakers!

This may also offer an explanation as to why I never completely identified myself with such a religious group. Although my mother and father claimed to be Christians as I was growing up, I was never raised in a group of firm believers or attended church on a consistent basis, so I never became part of a group that I couldn't let go of. This allowed me to look at religion objectively, instead of subjectively, and bring reason to the forefront without bias encoding. The short time I was involved with various churches, it was always music-related, and so I never really fell into the mass mentality—I was there to do a job and make music.

Christian, Muslim, Jewish, and other theistic children aren't so lucky. They inherit their parents' bias, and group activities, and by the time they can think for themselves, the group is a part of them—and they have an amazing desire to defend it, and a natural response to accept its mistakes, regardless of its metaphysical, magical, or outlandish claims that defy reality. They defend it as they would defend themselves.

# CHAPTER 6: MY CONVERSION?

## MY FRIEND, THE PREACHER

Early on in my journey, I met a preacher who became a true friend. We had similar senses of humor, similar family values, and enjoyed discussing numerous topics. Ironically, we hardly talked about religion for the first several years of our friendship. Circumstances changed, and we didn't talk for seven years. One day, I decided to email him to see if his contact information was the same, and surprisingly, he replied! By this time, I had discovered Atheism and realized that was the only option that made sense to me.

I told him of my Atheism, and he of course asked for the opportunity to convert me. I welcomed the 'help' he offered and agreed to review whatever evidence he had and attend his church services. He began sending things to me, and I was eager to learn.

Just a few days later, I received the evidence from my friend that the Christian god exists. I was looking at the exterior of the package, thinking of what he could have possibly sent. Was it something spiritual, or sentimental, such as a picture of his baby daughter, or are we really going to find hard evidence of the existence of the Christian god?

I opened the envelope to find two pamphlets, two books, and a video. The first thing that caught my attention was a colorful, brochure-looking document with a catchy title, which mentions an *Atheist sitting next to a preacher* ( I could not get permission to use the actual title in this book). At first glance, I was very excited. This seemed to be an interesting story of two men, forced to sit together on a long flight, debating the topic of religion. I was sadly disappointed when I realized the plane had landed by the end of the first page. The rest of the account was the preacher's thoughts and assumptions on what the Atheist *may have said* about various topics. I felt robbed. Regardless, I continued to read, because I promised my friend, the preacher.

The material went on to sarcastically slam Atheists and insinuate our lack of intelligence. I was a little shocked at the blatant arrogance portrayed. The writing as a whole was extremely slanted and biased toward the Christian faith. This was not science. This was only evidence that Christians have a different view than Atheists. I think we all already knew that, which essentially made this piece of evidence worthless. The author went on to mention it being *"safer to just believe; what do you have to lose?"* Yet the Christian belief posits that you must *know the Christian god to be true in your heart, and perform the will of the Christian god to enter the kingdom of Heaven.* Imagine that! I had opened just one piece of Christian evidence and already found a contradiction. I was really astonished by the next section, which was directed toward a younger audience. It specifically tells them to not be intimidated by educated Atheists. The material also shockingly says that evolution was actually *"disproved by science!"* I had to take a minute after reading that one. The scientific evidence for evolution is so overwhelming, it's now known as a fact, and accepted by on at least some level, nearly every religion, and endorsed by leaders all over the free world. I was really blown away by that blatant lie.

Near the end, as a final stab at Atheists, the author directly states in no uncertain terms that a man who believes in evolution does not have an ethical structure comparable to that of a creationist. My sincere thanks to the author; I'll never get those forty-five minutes back.

An important common denominator was starting to surface in this type of 'evidence.' It all seemed to begin with a slanted preface, defining the pivotal terms therein which could potentially be argued against. The authors were clear to set the stage in the beginning and tell me new meanings of words and actually pre-interpret what I was about to read—to be sure that I didn't mistakenly disagree with them. They took the time to change the vocabulary as I knew it to mean something completely different, in an attempt to set my mind thinking in a way that defies logic. Once the authors felt they had accomplished this, they moved forward with the depiction under the assumption that my view was now as skewed as theirs.

With that in mind, I began reading the second pamphlet, and learned that *creationism is actually closer to being considered scientific than evolution*! I was really having a hard time with this nonsense. Moreover, the theory that provides the most logical explanation by the end of this Christian reading should be considered proof. Then of course, the author defines logic for you in Christian terms, in case you have wrongly believed in Webster's definition. Despite the attempted foolery, the material did have a few important points that I feel I must address.

The single most convincing fact proposed in the reading was not proof that the Christian god exists but rather substantial evidence defying evolution. Simply put, in the many years paleontologists and other professionals have been searching, the pamphlet points out that very few actual bones have been collected. This is an incredible assertion that is made in complete blindness to the facts, and I can only point the reader toward any book on anthropology or to go online to www.talkorigins.com, which will quickly defuse this rumor.

The video my friend sent was nearly four hours long, and by judging the cover, it seemed to strongly promote finding the truth. In fact, the word truth was in the title. Finally, it was something we could agree on! I started to get excited once again and opened my mind to possible evidence. I was prepared to be converted. Yet, just as the pamphlets had projected a biased preface, the video contains the audio/visual equivalent. As it turns out, the video could have only been about three minutes long, because it immediately tells the viewer that the Christian god's word is the truth, and the Bible is absolute knowledge. Yes, I said *absolute*. They immediately lost me.

As for the theory that human life is too intricate and perfectly designed to be an accident, I'll say this: we wouldn't be here to discuss it if it hadn't happened at some point, so as amazing as it may be, it's not as improbable as many will have you think. There are billions of planets in the universe, and they've been around for billions of years. That means billions upon billions have failed at producing life. Just a small portion (roughly 26%) of *one* planet out of the billions we can see, actually produces life. There's no telling how many times there was a failed attempt just on earth to evolve life. In fact, 99% of the species that have existed are now extinct! That doesn't sound like a very intelligent design, but rather an incredibly high rate of failure. The simple notion that we are here today cannot be disputed. We are here. That doesn't make it a miracle; it just makes it a fact. Furthermore, the use of the word 'accident' is done so in a condescending manner by Christians, as to belittle the facts of evolution and cause one to subliminally feel that if you agree with evolution, your existence has a negative spin. Atheists do not believe this is true. Human life is precious and should be celebrated. It was not an accident; it was a natural, scientific progression that happened over such a large period of time, current minds have difficulty fathoming the possibilities of adaptation. That doesn't make it impossible.

The video openly portrayed the scare tactic theme, by showing car crashes, body bags, a funeral, and headstones marked "*Daddy*" and "*Mommy*" as the host (a preacher) walked through a cemetery with a Bible. One of the headstones even depicted a one-year-old child who had died. It was truly starting to turn my stomach. Up until this point, it had been an intelligent debate of two beliefs. This, however, is an attempt by Christians to use those who have perished as ammunition for their cause. I was sadly disappointed and quite angered.

The video also clearly points out where the Bible states "*few will enter the kingdom of Heaven, and many will be eternally punished*" (which I've discovered is why they call it being 'saved' when you accept Christ as your Lord). It seems as though you are primarily set on a path of destruction and damnation and are basically scheduled to be in Hell, unless you make a strong commitment to be 'saved.' However, even he who practices certain aspects of Christianity, professes Jesus as his savior, and attempts to live as perfectly as possible shall suffer the pain of eternal damnation if he does not *"do the will of the Father."* This video teaches that believing is not enough to enter Heaven (as does Matthew 7:21). In fact, according to the noted scriptures and all the professionals speaking on this video, one who lives righteously, confesses his sins, and requests to be baptized will still burn in Hell if the baptism isn't done properly. That's right! The sprinkle effect doesn't get the job done. Unless you are *"submersed in water, as Jesus was in the earth, you shall not enter the kingdom of Heaven."* Sorry, Catholics.

Wow. This sure sounds as though Christians are held to a much stronger set of rules than I once thought. If anything could be said about the Christian god at this point, it would have to be that he is unfair, tyrannical, and created billions of lives on Earth only to punish nine-tenths of them with eternal fire and damnation in the depths of Hell (*most, over a technicality*). I can honestly say if this is the god the Christians worship, even if he were proven true today, I would want no part of his rapture. I know if I haven't already, I'm about to offend all the Christians still reading this book. Honestly, this depiction of the Christian god just seems to make him more evil than good. How can you say otherwise? Why would a righteous god create this planet, and create precious human lives, knowing that a large majority of them will eternally suffer—just to be worshipped and praised? Why not just let it be? Is it really more important to create life for the sake of creation while knowingly causing billions of casualties, than to simply have peace alone? Would you personally have five children if you knew four of them were going to suffer a horrible burning death? What type of evil mind could create such a plan? It's simply horrific. Yet millions of people not only pray to this god every day, they believe he is watching every move they make, and is the living standard by which all morals should measure. It's a terrifying notion—and even more obvious that the Bible was written by archaic men that didn't really understand what they were talking about. The basis of religion was primitive man's first attempt at philosophy, geology, meteorology, and psychology, with no scientific evidence whatsoever. They were writing out of a fear for the unknown. They did the best they could, but Jesus Christ!—now we know better.

Christians consider this being as righteous and attempt to follow his every word, which was written and translated by man. I am astonished that much of this great country relies on the Bible and the Christian god depicted therein to create moral boundaries for society. Do they really know what they are following? At this point in my attempted conversion to Christianity, I was over half-way through the evidence, and even more convinced of my Atheism than ever before. Two actual books remained. Could these change my opinion?

As I began the first actual book, my fears were confirmed. Just as I suspected, the book's preface informed me on the very first page that unsuspecting students are often *swept onto the bandwagon* of evolution, and they don't quite realize they are being lied to. It refers to scientific facts as *"so-called evidence"* and says *evolution is not science, nor is it even a theory*! This author blatantly attacks evolution in a very sarcastic, unprofessional manner. I wasn't even sure I could finish this one. He was telling me how to think and how to read, before I ever got into the actual material. However, I did promise my friend the preacher that I would read the evidence with an open mind; but the prefaces offered in these readings and video want me to open my mind to the Christian way of thinking only and close my mind to the possibilities of science (which I trust on a daily basis for other things) disproving theology. I was hoping for facts presented to me in an unbiased manner. That clearly was not happening here, and I wasn't sure why I expected it at that point.

Basically, the author goes on to quote many other Christians, who happen to be educated in science. They all serve the same purpose—to point out the flaws in evolution that we have already discussed. Do you happen to remember that bully in school who couldn't show you his own personal confidence, so his alternative was to lower yours, thereby elevating his own using the process of elimination? I feel that's the tactic being used here. I am not seeing evidence of a god, let alone the Christian variation; I am only seeing the informal, unprofessional bashing of evolution. Christians are not working to find out more about the Christian god. They have simply stopped and accepted that whatever is in the Bible must be truth, and if you don't believe, you will be eternally punished. Meanwhile, they believe that if they can tarnish the reputation of evolution, as the bully did to the school children, creationism will somehow be elevated to the status of *truth* by process of elimination. Well, that only works on those that refuse to investigate.

The title of the second book looked promising. Although I had yet to open it, the cover didn't seem to bash evolution. It looked very scientific, and its title suggested evidence proving the existence of the Christian god. Should I have expected a slanted preface? I did not. I cleared my prejudice and cracked the book with an opened mind. While it seemed more professional, or less malevolent I should say, it still began under the assumption of the Christian god existing. There was no journey to seek the truth, no path to follow, and no evidence to sift through. It started off with the same assumptions, and it's more of an explanation of Christianity than proof of its correctness. The same story was told, the same evidence was presented—none of which was very convincing. Just 'telling' me that it's true isn't good enough, I was looking for evidence to make my own decision. It seems that these books have made up my mind for me, and they're just telling me what I now believe. Fortunately in my case, they were wrong.

## A SMALL RELIGIOUS TOWN

As I became more aware of the fallacies behind religions, especially Christianity, I wanted to know even more. I also wanted to share what I had learned with others. So, as I've eluded to in a previous section, I began a blog, (www.dogmadebate.com) where I posted random brief essays on my findings and offered a discussion board to get feedback from readers. One of those posts included the *"Top Ten Reasons I'm Atheist."* My friend the preacher read those reasons and created a full two-part sermon centered on refuting them. He sent me a message letting me know what he would be doing and included the address of his church. He probably never thought I would actually show up. If so, he was wrong.

After more than an hour driving on major interstates and toll roads, entering into Royse City, TX on a calm January evening is a bit like going back in time. It's a very friendly place, with people smiling, waving, and ready to welcome a visitor. It's the epitome of small-town America. I arrived about thirty minutes early on the outskirts of town (I've always wanted to use that phrase) and to my surprise, there was not a single Starbucks in the entire city! A nice lady at a convenience store tried to point me in the direction of a small coffee shop across the street, but I figured they wouldn't have my Tall Solo White Chocolate Mocha, so I headed directly to the church.

The preacher looked a bit surprised when I opened the door and walked in with my Bible in hand, and he greeted me with a smile and hug. He's truly one of the nicest people I've ever met.

The number of people to fill that category would be greatly increased as the night went on, as everyone seemed to be genuinely warm-hearted and welcoming of the visitor.

A small congregation of about thirty-five people gathered and took their seats, and I sat among them, just three rows from the front. The service began with 3 songs out of the 'Songs of Faith' book, and humorously, the final song before the lesson began was titled *I Am Thine O'Lord* and just happened to be #666 in the song book! (We later joked about that one, and the preacher assured me it was pure chance).

As the sermon began, the preacher never pointed me out or addressed me directly but only referred to me as "my friend the Atheist" during his presentation. His PowerPoint was very well put together, with each of my reasons projected on a large screen before the congregation. I vigorously took notes as he quoted other Atheists, scientists, and doctors, who basically agreed with my case and then refuted them with Bible scriptures and other 'evidence.'

## ATHEISM IN CHURCH

The feeling was a bit surreal as reason number one lit up the church wall. *"If we truly had one creator speaking to prophets, it would do so consistently; not contradictory as thousands of different religions have proven."*

The preacher answered this by saying he understands the confusion of many prophets, which is gathered by listening to men who worship false gods. Jesus essentially warned of this in the book of John, by saying this would happen if people didn't believe in him. The preacher also stated that the Bible was written in three different languages over sixteen hundred years by forty different men—yet it does not contain a single contradiction! He asserted that the book can be trusted to be the true description of messianic prophecies which described Jesus Christ, and therefore confirms its authenticity and infallibility. This was his reason for why the Bible should be trusted above all other holy books.

My first problem with this explanation was, of course, that many scholars have conceded multiple contradictions and fallible claims in the Bible. In fact, the very existence of Catholics, Baptists, and New Testament Christians alone are proof of contradictions, because each group interprets different meanings within the same scriptures. First Corinthians 14:33 states that *"God is not the author of confusion, but of peace."* If that were the case, there would be one Christian religion—one set of beliefs—one ethical code—and one way of worship—the correct, biblical one. But there are too many to count, due to the confusion. Besides, if I had to *tell* you that I'm not confusing, there's a problem to begin with. Things that are easily understood are self-evident.

My second problem was, claiming that all the other religious beliefs are focused on false gods is like saying "believe me because I said so." The Jews, Muslims, and Hindus all believe that Jesus was a false god. In fact, the Romans first called the early Christians "Atheists" because following Christ meant that *Christians* did not believe in the more common Roman polytheism of the time. I'm sure they would all have the very same 'truthful' claims about their own religion, and that all others are false. The preacher's refutation to my first reason for Atheism was really more basic religious rhetoric than reasonable evidential insights. He didn't provide any evidence to show the Bible was true, he simply *said* it was.

We then moved on to reason number two: ***Living by the means of man helping man, and realizing time on earth is not a practice run, creates an urgency of life that requires fulfilling.***

For this rebuttal, the preacher simply stated that he agreed with the notion of man helping man and that Jesus is actually the one who taught that lesson in Mark 12 when he said "love thy neighbor." The preacher was essentially faulting all "unbelievers" for following biblical teachings without belief in the Bible. The obvious problem with this statement is that time did not start with the book of Mark! How did humans ever make it as far as they did before the Bible was canonized, and before Jesus taught his lessons if he ever really taught them at all? Even if you believe the anti-scientific notion that the earth is less than ten thousand years old, how did people live for thousands of years before the Old Testament was written? Why didn't everyone run around killing each other? I will get to the other reasons the preacher addressed in just a moment, but I must pause to share with you a brief exchange we had after the sermon. The preacher wrote this in a short letter to me:

> *It's interesting to me that your morality, whether you're conscience of it or not, comes from the very Bible you reject. That's true for all Atheists.*" He later continued… "*Name ONE moral principle you have that's not in the Bible.*"

My full response follows:

*My Dear Friend the Preacher,*

> *Many of the moral principles we live by do appear in part or in whole, in biblical teachings; there is no argument there. But you act as if time started when the Bible was written.*
>
> *Many people were helping one another, loving their neighbors, refraining from rape and murder, and keeping each other in 'ethical check' long before the Bible came along—or we wouldn't have made it that far for the Bible to be written! Simply because the material appears in the Bible does not mean it is the absolute source of morality, or that it spawned ethics as we know it. We were not a bunch of raging cavemen until that set of scriptures was canonized. The Bible was*

*written by people who couldn't explain the source of their humanistic principles, so they assumed a god must have put them there.*

*But now that you've set the Bible on a pedestal of morals, let's have a look at it. Consider abortion. You have Christians on both sides of the argument, but what does the Bible say? Look at the death penalty. You have Christians on both sides of the argument, yet what does the Bible say? Look at homosexuality. You have Christians on both sides of the argument (including gay preachers, which neither of us understands) but what does the Bible say? The list goes on.*

*If Christianity were an absolute moral source, the followers of that religion should be consistent. Even the readers of the Bible don't agree on morality, so how can you say an Atheist lives by principles originated therein? Your Web-site alone criticizes Methodists and other religions for not living as you feel they should, but to them, they are living by 'God's word.' The crazy thing is, you're both right—and you can both prove it with scriptures!*

*I will take a moment to 'speak-Christian' and assume truths in the Bible in an effort to prove a point. Yahweh himself allegedly committed the most horrid acts found in this book you tell me to gain my morals from. In 1 Samuel 15:1–3 Yahweh orders the Israelites to attack Amalek, and says to kill "all men, women, infants, nursing children, ox, sheep, camels, and donkeys" out of revenge. Leviticus 24:10–16 shows that Yahweh had a man stoned to death simply for using his name in vain, and then made that a rule for everyone. In Second Chronicles 21:14–15 Yahweh cursed a man with a bowel disease that would eventually cause his intestines to fall out "day by day" as punishment for not "walking in the way of the Lord." In Second Kings 2:23–24 Yahweh has 42 children mauled by two bears, because they called Elisha "baldhead."*

*These few scriptures are in addition to the others I listed in my debate titled "For the Bible Tells Me So," where I've highlighted multiple stonings, burnings, and animal sacrifices that sicken those of us with humanistic principles, and could only be done so in the name of a religion. This is where you think modern day humans obtained our source of morality? Really?*

*It was Bruce Murphy (posting as Humanist-Dad) who said it best when he was asked to define the 'secular moral code' by an anonymous Christian on my debate site. His response was, "Philosophy, psychology, ethics, rational discourse, sociology... any discipline which adds to knowledge and finds good reasons for allowing or disallowing actions. Religious morality tries to declare actions right or wrong simply by saying that it is, or because an invisible, unknowable being says it is. We don't need this. We can figure out right from wrong ourselves."*

*We naturally choose the decision that causes the least amount of harm, and legally punish those who choose to infringe on others. That is the way of our society, and there's nothing religious about it.*

*During a recent conversation, I asked you if you could carry out the test given to Abraham in Genesis 22, where he is told to murder his child to prove his love for the Christian god. You said, "I know it would be the thing to do if God requested it, but I don't know that I would have as much faith or strength as Abraham did." That answer tells me that your humanistic principles are greater than the biblical morals you were taught—just as mine are.*

*You and I live by a similar code of ethics, but it is within us and is subject to our value-based decision-making—not controlled by the supernatural world. Saying that morals came from the Bible is like saying words originated from a dictionary. Both only recorded what already existed.*

*—David Smalley*

He never addressed this. My point was that the morals of Secular Humanists may appear in the Bible, but it doesn't mean they originated there. In fact, it really points to more proof that the Bible was written by people who could not describe their humanistic principles, so they assigned each a metaphysical source of creation. Humans had a decent nature to help one another survive long before the Bible came along, which is probably why we've made it so far in evolution. The fact that we're here attests to that.

Even more disturbing, was what the preacher said to his congregation regarding this second reason for my Atheism: *"If we take God and the Bible out of the equation, what obligation do we have to help our fellow man?"*

My answer, of course, is that we don't. There is no obligation—and frankly it's a sad thought to think Christians believe they need a god to tell them to be kind to each other. I briefly thought to myself "thank goodness for the myth of gods; otherwise, life with Christians may be unbearable!" Atheists don't help out because we feel forced; we do it because we understand the need for help and have felt that feeling of struggle. Through mirror neurons in the brain, we empathize with other creatures (especially our own species due to the evolution of the survival and compassion instincts) and usually want to minimize the pain and suffering of others. We understand that doing the least amount of harm to one another helps our species and furthers compassion, which prolongs our survival.

The preacher then said that I (his Atheist friend) basically felt like I had the power to create my own morality and rejected his god's. He said since there was no absolute authority, an Atheist can do whatever he desires. He then connected that by saying that Hitler thought he was doing the 'right' thing by exterminating the Jews and wondered aloud to the congregation *"How can an Atheist say that what Hitler did was wrong? By what authority is that measured?"*

I have a simple two part answer to that. For one, killing people causes a great amount of harm, and we wouldn't want to be killed, so we know it's not the best decision; and secondly, if I punched you in the face, would you need a pain-o-meter to say it hurt? How could you rightfully make the claim of another's pain without an accurate way to measure it?

My third reason for Atheism appeared on the giant wall: *I asked my four-year-old daughter where the stars came from. She confidently said "The moon made them." I followed by asking "Then where did the moon come from?" She strongly asserted "Daddy, the moon is the boss. Nobody made the moon." This is an unmistakably familiar mind-set and rightfully embarrassing for an adult to hold such similar thought.*

The preacher responded by saying that my daughter's mind-set was accurate, and that I should listen to her. Basically, he asserts that the Christian god has always existed. He quoted some scientists who admitted we did not know exactly how matter was created, but that we could only speculate certain theories. This, of course, is true, since no one was there at the moment everything began.

That answer to me, is intellectually tapping-out. Since we don't know what created the universe, we must assign a god to it. But the Christians go a step further. They claim to intimately know this god—what he wants, who he wants us to sleep with, what he wants us to eat, and what days he wants us to worship! This is repetitive of most monotheistic religions throughout history. When things can't be specified, or given a specific positive source, the archaic men of that time assign a god to the natural phenomena, and call it a day. It's referred to as the 'God of the Gaps,' and gaps are filled with glee by believers who don't want to search for the real answers.

As for the beginning of time, I will not pretend to know how it all started aside from the singularity causing the expansion of the universe; but my answer is that *we don't know yet*, not that *we need a god to explain it.* Assigning a god as the answer only begs more questions.

The preacher continued by saying it all comes back to the simple statement: "Something cannot come from nothing." I wanted the preacher to answer two simple questions, but I was unable to ask, so I will ask them here. Is the Christian god something? If yes, where did he come from? I could not stop the lesson and blurt that out as badly as I may have wanted to (just as I'm sure the preacher is reading this right now and wanting to blurt out of a few things of his own), but that was his time and I had to sit quietly and let him finish—this is mine.

The preacher continued to my fourth reason: *Demeter, Jesus, Apollo, Horus, Zeus, Mithra, Yahweh, Tammuz, Ganesha, and Allah are only ten of the thousands of gods recorded in history. An Atheist is not one who refuses to read religious doctrine; s/he is often one who reads too many.*

My friend the preacher paused to let it sink in, and then calmly said, *"Think about this one. Just because there is a counterfeit something, does that mean there is not a real one?"* My answer to that is no, of course not, but it does make one guess which is the counterfeit. He simply continued to repeat the rhetoric about Yahweh being the true god and that all other gods are false. He also pointed to more biblical scripture to prove his point. Muslims have scriptural proof that *Jesus* is a false god. Both books claim to be inspired by the one true god. My point is not to argue that Jesus wasn't real; my point was to show the many religious people across the world that wholeheartedly believe they are worshipping the true god, and all other god's are false, including the Christian one.

My fifth reason for being an Atheist appeared in church: ***In the technicalities of most religions, there is no difference between a believer who dies before having time to repent, and a nonbeliever who rejected the doctrine altogether.*** The Christian explanation for this one was that all people have time to repent. The preacher stated that according to the Bible, an 'unbeliever' is punished less than one who believes and then turns away from the church. The ideology behind this is, the more you know, the more you are responsible for worshiping Christ.

I found this to be very interesting, and very parental on the part of Yahweh. It seems that some rules are very specific, while some remain ambiguous. All people are given time to repent, but if you die as an 'unbeliever' you go to Hell. However, if you believe and then turn your back on the church, you go to Hell *worse*. I'm not really sure what that means, or how eternal damnation could be any worse; just like I am unclear about how those with mental illnesses get a 'special' place in Heaven, as though there is free parking or catered meals in the West Wing of Cloud 9!

These types of statements are just ridiculous. We are learning now that Heaven and Hell have degrees which get better or worse depending on what you do while you're here and are also affected by the way you were born, which you had no control over. As the preacher finished answering that reason, he again asserted that if you die before you accept Jesus as your savior, then you will go to Hell. Isn't that what I said to begin with? I was only more confused about the Christian position after his answer.

It became time for reason number six, which is one of my favorites: *If the Christian god created humans as sinners, how could it rightfully expect us to believe the corrupt messengers it has sent to teach us the way of life?* I am basically putting the preacher in the hot seat on this one, by asking, "How can I trust you, when you are a mere sinner?"

The answer the preacher gave is that the Catholics are essentially wrong, and we are not born sinners, and the Bible does not state that. He said *"Often times, Atheists and Agnostics are fighting against Catholicism, not Christianity."* He then pointed to biblical scriptures that prove that Yahweh created man "upright" and in his "own image" which is holy. This only perpetuated the confusion of the Bible, because Romans 5:12–14 clearly says this *"Therefore, just as through one man's sin entered the world, and death through sin, and thus death spread to all men, because all sinned. For until the law sin was in the world, but sin is not imputed when there is no law. Nevertheless, death reigned from*

*Adam to Moses, even over those who had not sinned according to the likeness of the transgression of Adam, who is a type of Him who was to come."* Once again, the Bible has not let us down in proving both sides of a disagreement to be correct.

The preacher then pointed out my use of the word 'it' when referring to the Christian god and wondered if it was intentional or had malice. He went on to say he thinks I am very angry with the Christian god for some reason, which he felt became clearer in my last reason for Atheism.

I had no intention of offending Christians with my use of the word 'it.' But what makes a man a man? A man is human, and a woman is human, and each have attributes which separate them from one another. Nothing can be a man and not be human. Yahweh is not said to be a human, so how could it be a man? I typically refer to the Christian god with male pronouns simply because the Bible does, but I'm never really sure how to address gods as it pertains to their gender. If I do refer to them in gender-specific language, I am thinking of them as characters in books and in the minds of humans, just as I would address Peter Pan as a boy, although he is not a human at all. But Yahweh has no real gender; therefore, 'it' should not be offensive to Christians.

The seventh reason was a direct quote from Epicurus: ***"Is God willing to prevent evil, but not able? Then He is not omnipotent. Is He able, but not willing? Then He is malevolent. Is He both able and willing? Then whence cometh evil? Is He neither able nor willing? Then why call Him God?"*** Essentially, the array of ancient comments and questions break down to force the Christian apologists to explain the existence of bad things happening, as does the problem of evil. The preacher began by saying that 'God' created people in an innocent form but gave them a choice. When people choose against this god, evil happens. He blames four basic principles for the existence of "evil." (1) Our own personal choices. (2) The personal choices of others. (3) The personal choices of generations past. (He gave Adam and Eve as an example, and said all of our suffering is due to them "violating the will of God." This is of course referring to them eating from the Tree of Knowledge of Good and Evil). (4) Natural laws that 'God' put into effect. He ended by saying that good can come from suffering because sometimes people better themselves upon going through tribulations.

Of course, numbers one and two are correct. Bad things happen because people choose to do bad things. The point Epicurus was making was "why is evil a choice at all?" That's equivalent to me placing a cookie within reach of a three-year-old girl and telling her not to touch it, and then spanking her when she does. As the adult, I could have prevented her suffering by removing the temptation. According to the preacher's logic, we don't really have 'free will,' as he suggests, but instead, we are created by a powerful being without our choice, baited like animals, and then tortured beyond belief if we fail the test. It's an absurd notion, and sounds more like a killer whale toying with its prey than a righteous god interacting with his proud creation.

His lack of reasoning concerning Adam and Eve is even more ridiculous. Because one woman and one man ate from a tree over 2,000 years ago, we are supposed to inherit a life of pain, sickness, shame, and death. The entire world was perfect until they ate the fruit. Can you really say that with a straight face? This seriously sounds like a fairy tale and is frankly laughable. First of all, for Yahweh to continue to punish us thousands of years after one mistake was made by our ancestors is unfair to say the least. Secondly, if Adam and Eve were *truly* perfect, why would they have made the *wrong* decision? They would have had no concept of 'death' which Yahweh threatens them with if they eat from the tree, and no concept of 'doing wrong' would have been existent within them if they were perfect. It boggles the mind that people actually believe in a talking snake that convinced a woman to eat a fruit, who convinced a man, and that's why we get cancer! Where's the logic and how is faith formed from that nonsense?

The natural laws he refers to are simply that—natural laws. I'm not sure how that applies to evil, and he didn't really elaborate. If we visit his answer more closely, we see that his short answer seems to be that evil is what happens when we choose against the Christian god. This is interesting, and it makes me wonder how he defines the 'evil' that is done in the name of the Christian god. Killing homosexuals, killing adulterers, and suppressing women's rights all fall under 'bad' in the vocabulary of most. Yet each of these is now, or at one time were the 'will of God.' There is no denying that; after all, it's evident in the scriptures which he continuously points to as proof, and the infallible word of his god.

The eighth and most controversial reason lit up the church wall next. *All babies are Atheists. Religions are taught depending on the location and era in which you are raised. Being born in the U.S. in 1972 does not make you right, it most likely just makes you another Christian. That's no better or worse than the*

**person born in Tibet in 1952, who proudly worships the Dalai Lama.**

The first sentence created a bit of a 'gasp' from a few church members, and rightfully so. This is a small Christian town, where most of the population really didn't understand what an Atheist was and had certainly never met one until just minutes before this lesson started. Like me, most of them had been raised to think of Atheists, infidels, and heathens as very bad and evil people. To call a baby an 'Atheist' in church was culture shock to say the least.

The preacher quickly addressed the first sentence, by saying that babies aren't born "anything," including Christian. He concludes that babies are not taught to sneeze, they are not taught to blink, and they have some things that are just "programmed" in them, which implies a "programmer." He continued by saying; *"Since Atheism is a belief system, and babies do not believe anything, a baby can't be born into Atheism. I'd like to know how my friend the Atheist arrived at that conclusion."* I wanted to jump up and say it right then, but again, I remained seated and silenced out of respect.

If Atheism is a belief system, then 'sitting down' is an exercise! Atheists do not follow any system of beliefs. We simply reject the unprovable claims of religions. Atheists have no personal concept of gods at all; nor do babies. All babies are born Atheists because they have the same amount of belief in a deity that I do—none. The word 'god' means the same to me as it does to a baby. Do you see the correlation? Religions are taught as we grow older, and theists are simply a product of the time and place in which they are born, and most likely, the beliefs of their parents are handed down as they are taught to fear whatever they know to be 'God.'

On to reason nine: *It is better to find your own answers and make an educated decision than to intentionally remain uneducated and make a fearful one.*

For this one, he actually agreed. It was simple and to the point. He wanted his children to make up their own minds by looking at the "evidence." Then he said he has to teach his children the will of the "Father." Wait a minute! If children are programmed with specific fundamentals like sneezing and blinking, why aren't they programmed to know the "Father?" This is a lack of logic on the part of Christians, and again, they will say it's because "he wants us to have free will." But just knowing that Yahweh exists would not force us to follow him—one only needs to understand the story of Satan to realize this. You see, in the story of Christianity, Satan knew who Yahweh was, and turned against him. Therefore, we could still have a choice even knowing the god of the Bible exists. The entire concept here becomes illogical.

My final reason for Atheism: *Only for the sake of argument, if I were to astonishingly find myself face to face with a supreme being, I would expect to be judged on my life as a humanist, and how I treated others (just as most Christians plan to be judged on character, not on the actual Ten Commandments). If my positive actions were ignored, and I was instead judged on using my intelligence to doubt religious doctrines created by human sinners, I would rather be eternally punished than bow to such an unfair tyrant who made things seemingly impossible for humans to succeed at this horrific game.*

The preacher refuted the first part of my statement by making the case that the creature does not set the expectation of judgment, but the creator does. I suppose he would have me here, and it's really my fault for roaming into the whole 'sake-of-argument' debate to begin with. I should have left that one alone and stuck to nine reasons. But since I put it out there, I must defend my position. I was basically just saying that one would hope that a super-intelligent being that created all of us would have enough reason and logic himself to look at the whole picture of people's lives and realize that they are not  bad; and instead would only punish the ones that murdered, raped, and caused harm. It was silly of me to even argue the possibility of there being a god in the first place, but knowing what I know about the biblical accounts of Yahweh, it really wouldn't surprise me if he *did* focus on technicalities and cursed my soul with some sort of bowel disease! The preacher is completely right here, it was my fault for wandering into his magical land of fiction with a reasoned approach.

He continued by saying that Christians are not under the 'Ten Commandments,' because Jesus Christ died for the sins of man. I don't think many Christians are aware of this.

He called the second part of my comment both "sad" and "shocking" and read it aloud again very slowly to add drama: *"If my positive actions were ignored, and I was instead judged on using my intelligence to doubt religious doctrines created by human sinners, I would rather be eternally punished than bow to such an unfair tyrant who made things seemingly impossible for humans to succeed at this horrific game."* After a long pause, he dramatically said, *"Do you see the anger in there? That's probably why my friend the Atheist called God 'it' earlier."*

As I previously stated, I can have no anger for something I do not acknowledge. My statement is simply designed to make the point that Christians have been given an impossible task, with reason and logic embedded in them, and instead of worshipping this being, they should be investigating its existence because nothing all-good and all-knowing would treat its creation so pitifully.

The preacher closed by repeating my rebellious words even slowler and more dramatically than before as the room became uncomfortable: *"I would rather be eternally punished than bow to such an unfair tyrant."* Then he looked directly at me and calmly said, *"Be careful what you wish for."*

You could have heard a pin drop. Everyone knew at that moment, that I was his friend—the Atheist. I smiled at him. It was intense—for everyone but me. By this time, I was completely comfortable with the fallacies in the Christian belief system and utterly open about my Atheism. I have no fear of the supernatural, and it shows in my confidence in approaching these matters with a logical framework as opposed to a fearful demeanor of faith.

The preacher then invited anyone who wished to join and accept Christ, to do so right then, and added that the baptism could take place at that moment. He ended, as all Church of Christ preachers seem to do, with the words: *"The choice is yours, while we stand and while we sing."*

I couldn't help but feel all eyes on me, as the congregation wondered if the sermon had suddenly created a change of heart in me. I must admit, I felt a lot of pressure at that point and just had so much to say to the preacher, I didn't know where to begin. To be honest, I didn't want it to be over. I wanted to know more, and

I wanted more explanations. With the end of the song, the service was over, and everyone began to mingle.

It didn't take long before I was approached with many handshakes and comments of *"thanks for coming."* I was never defiant in any way. At one point, a nice lady came up to me and said, *"thanks for worshipping with us."* I politely said *"Well, I really came to learn more about Christianity."* I wanted to make it clear that what I had just done was not 'worship,' but tolerance and educational. Then, just as if I had come for snacks and a movie, I saw the preacher's wife and kids, and we talked about old times for a few minutes as the congregation dissipated.

After the lesson, the preacher and I spent two hours in a conference room debating scriptures and topics which we both thoroughly enjoyed. I would have rather done that in front of his congregation, but his goal was not to make a scene. He truly wanted to convert me. Here is what I briefly learned about my friend, the preacher that I did not know.

- He does not celebrate Christmas as the birth of Christ. He noted 'Christ + Mass' is a formula which derived as a Catholic adaptation of pagan holidays celebrating the Winter Solstice. He rightfully said that no one knows when Jesus was born, and celebrating Christmas is not in the Holy Bible.

- He does not celebrate Easter as the resurrection of Christ. That too, he stated, is a Catholic ritual.

- He does not think we are all born sinners. In his interpretation, that's not in the Bible, so it's not consistent with his teachings, and is again, a Catholic adaptation.

- He only supports Old Testament teachings as 'lessons' but not to live by in this day and age. He follows the New Testament.

- He *does* support 1st Corinthians 14:34–35 which states that women should keep silent in church, and 1st Timothy 2:11 which states women should not teach nor be in positions of authority.

## THE LIVE DEBATES

By this point it would be hard to consider myself still on a journey, but rather on a mission of civil rights. I had not only accepted Atheism wholly but began to defend the materialistic position that Christianity lacks sufficient proof, yet boasts of entitlement to control society and legislate for the citizens of the United States. I felt they should have more proof than just their own faith before they start to make laws to control human behavior.

I joined the organization American Atheists, Inc. in 2007 and began contributing articles as a writer of the *American Atheist*, the organization's monthly magazine. I later became the designer, adding graphics and building the magazine, and was ultimately promoted as the youngest person to ever hold the title of Editor of the publication, at the age of 29.

Due to the announcements and publicity that come with such a title, I was engaged on multiple levels by preachers, talk-show hosts, bloggers, and other writers on topics of religion. I welcomed such scrutiny myself and enjoyed the banter. I, too, engaged those of the opposite persuasion, often calling into conservative or Christian radio stations and debating live on the air. I was ultimately invited to join Dr. Barry Creamer on his Dallas/Ft. Worth FM Christian radio show *Live From Criswell* and humbly accepted. I often heard him speaking on the air, and he seemed to be a very logical and impartial man, unusual for a Christian talk-show host. He, of course, was conservative on political views but often debated as the 'devil's advocate' when other conservatives called in. I enjoyed this about his show but suddenly realized things were treated very differently when religion was the topic and an Atheist was opposite him. There was hardly indifference. With his PhD in Humanities, and a very long resumé as a preacher in multiple churches, Dr. Creamer constantly showed that he knew his Bible, believed the words wholeheartedly, and would defend it to its core. I couldn't wait to get on the air with him.

I arrived at the studio a little early and was welcomed by his producer, Daisy, who was very nice in offering me a bottle of water and nonreligious conversation while we waited for Dr. Creamer to arrive. After a quick tour of the studio and a sound check, we were ready to go.

Dr. Creamer and I got along very well, and I quickly discovered that we had a common interest. Much to my surprise, he too was interested in Brazilian jiu-jitsu, in which I had competed in tournaments and trained for a few years before my schedule no longer permitted it. Nevertheless, I had a job to do, and he was both my interviewer and my opposition. I knew this was going to be a good time, and it was.

We did five consecutive interviews, all of which were pre-recorded. The playback was a little unfair in my regard, but I knew what I was getting into and accepted it. Dr. Creamer, who is a professor at Criswell College (a Baptist Seminary in Texas), invited another professor, Dr. Joe Wooddell, a professor of philosophy at the same campus, to join him on the air for the 'reviewing' of my pre-recorded sessions.

At the point of airing, I was no longer in the studio. And each Monday for five consecutive weeks, I sat in traffic on my way home with all the listeners, as the interviews were played and the two Dr.'s analyzed my difficult world view for all of Dallas to hear.

The first listener email was sparked by Dr. Creamer simply saying that I was a "nice guy." The man wrote in and actually accused me of being the embodiment of the Anti-Christ and condemned the host for complimenting me! The email said that Satan was using "nice Mr. Smalley" to "pull us all in." He posted his comments on Dr. Creamer's Web-site, so I responded directly to him with the following written message:

*Dear Listener,*

*Let me start by saying that I understand your concern, and realize that scripturally, you have valid points. After all, it is Matthew 12:30 that says, "He who is not with me is against me..." and Mark 9:40 that says, "for whoever is not against us is for us." I do not take your animosity personally, as I understand it is your religious convictions and faith that lead you to believe the way you do. I will not hold that against you, as I understand how powerful that can be.*

*What I stand for, is more of a civil rights issue than a religious one. You should know that if the U.S. President announced today that Christianity was no longer allowed to be practiced in this country, I'd be on the picket lines with you, fight-*

*ing for your constitutional rights, and freedom of religion. I do not wish to see a complete banishment of Christianity. I do, however, want to stand for the freedom of all citizens in this country, and prevent the discrimination of all people, regardless of their religious views. This was intended to be a free country, not a Christian nation.*

*My children should not have to go to a public school and be ridiculed for not believing. Families should not be separated with members ostracized due to religious convictions. Qualified applicants should not be turned down for government jobs due to a lack of belief. A person should not be considered "unethical" until they identify with a religion. But why do we debate? The whole point here is, the Atheist says to all religions, "Before you will control my government, my family, or my career, you need to supply more proof than just faith."*

*I must also point out that the "A" in Atheist does not represent "Anti" or "Against," but rather "without." The theist holds a belief in a deity, while the a-theist is without that belief. It's really that simple. Saying that an Atheist is the opposite (or anti) any particular religion is like saying a doctor is the opposite of a disease. He studies it, and fights it from time to time, but also respects its power, while questioning its intent.*

*We stand aside from all belief systems, (including Satanic ones) saying each is without sufficient proof. As Dr. David Eller confirms in his book* Atheism Advanced, *the Atheist is more of one that discredits religions than opposes them directly (2007).*

*Mr. Hardt, people can be nice without religions. Adults can debate without hate. Opening the educational views on the airwaves of 90.9 KCBI allows Christian listeners to better deal with Atheists they encounter, and vice versa for Atheists encountering Christians. More than anything, it was important for listeners to hear an educated conversation between two men that disagreed without anger. If we had more of that, I honestly think the world would be a better place.*

*I'm not sure what you did last night, but I took my children out to eat at Logan's Roadhouse, where we threw peanut shells on the floor, and ate desert out of tiny peanut buckets. I tucked my five-year-old daughter into bed at nine, and realized that I forgot a permission slip for my son to play basketball at school, resulting in an email to his teacher begging for forgiveness.*

*I managed to have two solid hours of phone conversations with Christian preachers that are very good friends of mine, one of which I am debating soon. Once the kids were asleep, I continued my research into PhD programs that I plan to attend very soon.*

*My life isn't much different from yours, aside from what we consider to be proof of a religion. I just don't trust that what those men wrote as scriptures was inspired by something powerful, other than their own hopes and beliefs.*

*I assure you, I don't have time to be the Anti-Christ—and I can't imagine it paying very well at all.*

—*David Smalley*

Despite that one strange encounter and unique perception, the overall reaction was very good. The callers were extremely interested in my world view, and the host was too—although at times it felt more like an interrogation than an interview! As I listened to the response of the doctors analyzing my comments, I wanted so badly to call in and participate. But I had promised that I would allow the Christians to have a field day with my comments, and so I did.

The assertions of *"I think David Smalley would say..."* and *"he probably thinks that..."* were at times a bit frustrating, because they often spent time chasing a rabbit that I would have

Baptized Atheist

never released, down holes that I didn't know existed. In fact, at one point, the visiting professor, Dr. Wooddell, said, *"Why didn't he research Christianity before making up his mind? Why didn't he read the very best, like C.S. Lewis, or Lee Strobel!?"* For those that don't know, both of these authors were once Atheists and later converted to Christianity. Therefore, they have been monumental in Christian apologetics from a former-atheistic perspective. That's why it was so important to the radio hosts that I looked into these men who had 'seen the light' and read their words carefully.

After just the first show, with four more weeks to go, I was chomping at the bit to get back on the air because material like that is exactly what I had been researching for the last thirteen years. I read C.S. Lewis' *Mere Christianity* and *The Problem of Pain* along with Lee Strobel's *The Case for the Real Jesus*, Christopher Hitchens' *God is Not Great: How Religion Poisons Everything*, and Richard Dawkins', *The Greatest Show on Earth: the Evidence for Evolution*—not to mention, that one very important book, *The Holy Bible*! I had also read *The Bible Handbook* by W.P. Ball (*et al.*) which proposes multiple contradictions in biblical texts, followed by *Alleged Bible Contradictions Explained*, a Christian apologetics book by George W. DeHoff. Further, I had specifically chosen psychology with an emphasis in *applied behavioral analysis* as my educational field of study to get a better understanding of why people acted the way they did and how our brains really worked to produce thoughts and beliefs.

I had spent the majority of my time listening to Christian radio and privately debating with Christian preachers from multiple denominations to get a clear understanding of Christianity as a

210

whole system of beliefs. I had literally dedicated my life to researching Christianity and had written over 80 published articles and blogs on the topic and roughly 90% of this book by the time I did these interviews, but was being accused live on FM radio of doing no such thing.

I was promised a chance to rebut these things on the air and eagerly awaited my turn. In order to continue my effort of being chronologically consistent with my life, I must come back to that in a moment. For it was during this wait to get back on the radio that I was challenged to a live debate by a reader of mine, Michael Hildreth.

The man making the challenge was a Church of Christ preacher, who proposed a debate at the Seagoville Church of Christ and wanted to debate me in front of a largely Church of Christ congregation with another Church of Christ preacher as the moderator. I felt sorry for my prospective opponent that the odds would be so deeply stacked against him!

Many of my colleagues refuse to debate Creationists at all, but I must make a clear stand for why I encourage it. Simply put, it raises awareness. It educates the believers on what Atheists actually stand for, and that we are not some horn-growing, tail-waving, fire-spitters out to destroy our country. It's important for them to see into our world just a little, and who knows, one closet Atheist among the congregation or university may come to a realization that he or she no longer needs to hide. That's why I eagerly accept nearly every debate offered to me.

Three hours into our first meeting at an *On the Border* Mexican restaurant in Plano, Texas, (paid for by the great and powerful

Mr. Bill Burk) the deal was done. We had agreed upon a time line, structure, debate proposition, and evidence that would be presented. We were all looking forward to it.

When the day finally arrived, I must admit that it was a bit surreal. I was sitting on a stage in a beautiful church, smelling that wonderful church smell as the crowd looked on. It brought back fond memories of playing drums for the choirs and having lunch in the back room after the sermons. Although this wasn't the exact church I had been in as a child, I was very comfortable in this setting. The preacher was at the podium making his case for the existence of the Christian god, and I was looking around, holding my Bible, knowing that I was just minutes away from standing behind that pulpit myself to present evidence that the god these people pray to every day doesn't exist. Surprisingly, I wasn't a bit nervous.

And just like that, it was my turn. They had all heard his rhetoric before. It's the same argument. "God exists because the Bible says so, and we should trust the Bible because it's the word of God, and we know that because the Bible is infallible." It's that spinning circle of reasoning power that traps those of faith and makes those with reasonable logic nauseous and dizzy. It was time to hear the Atheist speak in church.

My argument was based on the fact that Jaycee Dugard, an eleven-year-old girl, was kidnapped in 1991 and raped and abused for 18 years before being rescued. I looked into the eyes of as many congregation members as I could and asked them, "Did God watch?" It was uncomfortable, but necessary. I needed to point out that this glorious, powerful, good, and all-knowing being that they celebrate every Sunday morning is the same ultimate reality that apparently watches the torture and abuse of innocent children yet chooses to do nothing about it. I wanted them to think back and remember how many Sundays had passed with them singing praises to their all-mighty creator, and bellowing out how great he is, while Jaycee was suffering in agony in a shed behind a house, begging to be let go. Do you think any of them counted the Sundays that passed during this time? I did; it was 936. The crowd sat silently, partially angered, partially enlightened, and partially confused—all of which were the desired effect.

During the intermission I looked over and noticed my opponent didn't have anything to drink. I had brought some extra waters with me and noticed how incredibly dry my mouth was from speaking for a solid thirty minutes and knew his must have been the same. So I took one across the stage to him, and he quickly accepted, complaining of thirst. He joked about it being "laced with something," we had a laugh, and I returned to my side of the stage. Interestingly enough, he used his next time at the microphone to claim that I had no source of morality, so that proved that I must have been "okay with the suffering that happened to Jaycee Dugard!" The irony was compelling.

As the debate went on, and I challenged the talking animals and atrocities in the Bible, my opponent admitted a few things that were quite funny to me. He alluded to the fact that it makes more sense for a snake to talk than to say we "came from a snake!" I was a bit surprised that he logically and seriously admitted that a snake would speak, but even more so, I was in awe that he had not so much as read a single article on evolution prior to the debate, or he would know that evolution makes no such claim. As you know from Chapter 4 in this book, evolution states that all things share common ancestors, not that we 'descended' from anything living today. For some reason, I don't think that made much of a difference for the audience. If you'd like to view the actual video, it's available from my Web-site.

As the debate ended, I was approached by many of the audience members who thanked me for coming. I remember one sweet elderly woman who shook my hand, touched my arm, and said, *"I know this doesn't mean anything to you, but I'll be praying for you."* My response was simple, *"I know what it means to you to add me to your prayers, and I thank you for keeping me in your thoughts."* I am not one of those Atheists who become offended by prayer; it's when believers rely solely on that for cures, success, parenting, and assistance that frustrates me to no end. Over all, the mood was relaxed. One gentleman, who was at least seventy, firmly shook my hand and said, *"Young man, you have been very educational, and I appreciate you coming."* I took that as a very big compliment and appreciated everyone's hospitality.

Ironically, the only person who treated me with disrespect was my good friend the preacher, from Chapter 6! Yes, he showed up, sat in the back, and nudged his friend and laughed when I said something he didn't agree with. Several times he made eye contact with me as I was speaking and shook his head in disagreement. It was rude, distracting, and unprofessional, but I did not let that spoil my night or my position. I also knew that he was not a representation of the church as a whole, and I would never make that statement or assumption. It never threw me off course, but I was disappointed because I had expected more of him as a friend. When I questioned him about this behavior, he admitted to me that since I became an Atheist, he had always seen our friendship as *superficial* and honestly considered me an enemy. I was shocked to learn this, but it explained a lot of his actions. Not a single stranger treated me with disrespect, and over all, it was a wonderful time we had together. I had lost one friend, but gained many.

One week after the live debate, I was headed back to the studios of *Live from Criswell* to offer my response to the five weeks of callers and Christian Doctors who analyzed my prerecorded interviews. Only this time, I was to be live on the air responding to the comments and taking even more live callers. Several questions were posed for me to address as Christian listeners all over the Dallas/Ft. Worth area struggled to understand the Atheist position.

The first question that really caught my attention was presented by the philosophy professor, Dr. Wooddell, who was there to help Dr. Creamer analyze my interviews. He mentioned my work with the homeless, and my plans to begin a nonprofit organization, and said *"If you're going to help someone in the name of... I don't know what..., that's a problem in itself!"* This one was quite disturbing to me. To think that this educated man actually believes that in order to help someone, you must do so "in the name of something" is just preposterous. UNICEF is a major organization known to be in 191 countries helping children all over the world overcome disease and starvation, and they proudly assert themselves as a secular organization. The American Red Cross (despite Bill O'Reilly's false claim that the cross was adopted as a result of Christianity), is also a secular organization focused on helping individuals in need—especially in times of disaster. The bottom line here is that a *belief* is not required to recognize hunger, pain, sadness, disease, and poverty. The desire to help also works fine without belief as a prerequisite. It was Albert Einstein who said, *"If people are good only because they fear punishment, and hope for reward, then we are a sorry lot indeed."* Regardless of how much I mention it, or otherwise chose not to, my work with the less fortunate is in no way diminished by my lack of belief in any certain deity. One only needs to research Secular Humanist organizations to see this in action.

It was the show's host, Dr. Creamer, who dropped the next bombshell. When basically challenging my moral and ethical foundation, as often happens in exchanges like this, he finally said the words I'd been waiting on someone to say: *"I have the Ten Commandments to tell me what's right and wrong."* That seems to be easy to say and is typically the final words of a conversation over ethics with a Christian. But I didn't let it stop there. That deserves to be challenged for two simple facts. First, the commandments in the Bible are obviously not absolute, because the Christian god chooses to break some of them on multiple occasions and excuses his own behavior based on his judgment as the Creator. If it's based on judgment, it's not absolute and is really just based on his opinion (which is a strange coincidence, because using my own judgment is the very reason I'm accused of being immoral). Secondly, the Ten Commandments can't possibly deal with every moral situation that we will encounter. In fact, the first four commandments only deal with how you should worship and make no ethical reference whatsoever. The last six are simply: *honor your parents, don't murder, don't cheat on your spouse, don't steal, don't lie,* and *don't covet* (or deeply desire) *anything that someone else owns.* So which of these can we use to determine whether or not to park in a handicap spot when we're in a hurry? That would obviously be unethical, but it's not addressed in any way in the Bible. Which commandment am I following when I knock on my neighbor's door to remind him his garage door is open, or when I help the sweet elderly woman across the street change the batteries in her smoke detectors? What do these really have to do with commandments or divinely inspired ethics? Moreover, while the commandments specifically teach *against* murder, murder is also *commanded* throughout the Bible by Yahweh. So obviously, murder for certain despicable crimes (like working on the Sabbath day or being gay) is acceptable. Therefore, it confuses the moral position of the death penalty, and that's why we see Christians on both sides of that moral dilemma.

The Bible should never be confused with an absolute set of morals for these reasons, but so many people, even those with graduate degrees and years of education on Christianity, still cling to it as such. So when your seventeen-year-old neighbor comes knocking on your door in the middle of the night as a run-away, and you're faced with that moral decision to either call her parents immediately or just talk her through the hard times; consult that fountain of knowledge [*sic*] that is the Ten Commandments, and see what answer it provides you.

A caller named Jason said, *"How does David Smalley classify evil?"* This is one of the more simple questions, but a powerful one for Christians to hear the answer to. I only needed to ask in return, *"What if I walked into a strange town and wiped out an entire neighborhood, killing men, women, and infant children—would you call that evil?"* Everyone undoubtedly answers "yes," just as the preacher and the caller both did on the air. Then I simply responded with *"that's what the Christian god commanded in the Old Testament; what is he?"* The surprise rings a bell for most, but I still feel the need to answer the question from my Atheistic perspective. I continued: *"Evil has multiple definitions, none of which are very meaningful, but it still does not exist in spiritual form, (*as I stated in Chapter 5). *Therefore, we can only categorize the things we don't agree with as 'bad' or 'evil,' but nothing in the evil category is absolute or pure."* I can only answer this by saying that which causes undue harm to innocent individuals could be considered evil, but according to the dictionary a smell could be evil if it doesn't comport with what we think smells good.

Another caller, who also showed up to the live debate, sat in the front row, and seemed to be uncontrollably drawn to my blog with a mission to convert me by verbal force, was named Denese. Once on the air, she said: *"David Smalley and other Atheists are very religious in their 'no God.'"* This led Dr. Wooddell to add that Atheists start with faith in their senses, just as Christians begin with faith in 'God,' and in that respect must be considered among the faithful.

Many Atheists seem to be annoyed by the word faith, and this is probably why so many Christians use it to describe us. It's sort of in the realm of 'you're no better than me' and uses that word 'faith' in an attempt to equate Atheism with a religion. While Atheism is certainly not a religion, the word 'faith' really doesn't bother me as much as it does many of my colleagues. I prefer not to use the word *faith* only because of the more common meaning it holds and would rather say that I have 'confidence' in my senses, or 'trust' in science to prove things. But realistically, faith, confidence, and trust, ultimately share meanings in different texts. If we try to run from the word *faith* altogether, it only looks like we are stretching the English language just as we accuse the theists of doing, and we become apologists or spin doctors to try and talk our way out of having faith while still conceding trust and confidence. Then, they are right, our logic is no better than theirs.

I choose not to play that game. One variation of the word *faith* does include trust in an outcome, and in that respect, I do have trust. The primary difference is what lies at the basis of that trust. The Atheistic claim is on past, factual experience, while Christian faith is built on dogmatic assertions. That's why we can't pretend that all faith is equal, as I explained in Chapter 4 when I described my Faith-o-meter Theory. For example, if I say that I have faith that the sun will be visible tomorrow, you know exactly what that means and must concede that the odds are in my favor by process of induction (which is a generalization from past experiences). Still, because we have not seen the sun yet again—and conditions may not be the same in places that we can't measure, there is a small amount of faith involved in expecting that it will be visible tomorrow. But again, this is using the 'trust' or 'confidence' variation of the word, not to be equated with the 'hope in a magic god' variation. We're all pretty sure it's going to happen, but since it hasn't happened yet, there is a bit of confidence, or faith, or trust that is required until we have all the evidence and the sun is actually visible. However, when Christians say they have "faith in God," that's not quite as clear. What does it actually mean? Is it really fair to say that faith in the sun shining tomorrow is the same as faith in a mystical creature that no living person has ever seen? Of course not; there are obviously different levels of trust as different levels of evidence are introduced. Then, we just get into a battle of semantics over what *faith* means, and we both just become apologists for our respective causes because there are multiple definitions for the word, ranging from *trust* to *godly relationships*. We typically hear of faith in the latter sense, so Atheists tend to shy away from it, and I agree with this notion. But when faced with a dictionary, we can't hide from it very long. It's better to face it head-on and describe the differences between the levels and meanings of faith than to deny we have it altogether. We do occasionally have trust in results, and we can't get out of that.

When the caller said we were religious, perhaps she was referring to the evangelical mission many Atheists seem to be on (such as myself) doing interviews, and writing blogs and books. Well, there's one major difference between our message and those of the religious. It's more defensive than offensive. We aren't saying, "join us or suffer," we're saying "you don't have sufficient proof for your claims, so you're not going to control our lives or force legislation upon our governments." If that outspoken message (that is actually a stance for civil rights) appears to be evangelical, then so be it. I really don't care what you call it. But I have no amazing after-life or promise to offer those that choose Atheism, and I certainly do not promise any sort of eternal damnation for those that disagree with me. That would be religious, and religious I am not.

So why do we Atheists have *confidence* or *faith* or *trust* in our senses? Why do we trust that when we see something it's real, and when we touch something, it's actually there and not a dream? As Dr. Wooddell stated, *"How does David Smalley know he's not in a padded room, and life is all just a dream?"* Again, this is a bit of a stretch, and even if I failed miserably at my explanation, it didn't prove that Christianity is the one true system to follow. But after all, I had submitted myself to this Christian radio show and agreed to answer the questions, so I continued.

My response was simple: The brain is our only natural tool for measurement. We have to trust it. If we throw that out, there's no point in having any discussion about anything, ever. If *trusting our brain because our brain has proven itself trustworthy* can be considered circular reasoning, then I suppose *trusting a ruler to be 12 inches long because it is in fact, 12 inches long,* is also circular reasoning! At some point we have to at least agree on the tools for measurement, or you're just having a philosophical discussion that becomes a whirlwind of nonsense with counter arguments such as *"well how do I know that you just said that? Until you can prove you just spoke, I don't need to respond!"* That could go on for hours, until the listeners or readers are either asleep, or have forgotten the topic we were discussing.

So why do I trust my senses? It's simply because it's the only tools we are equipped with which to measure facts. And if I'm tasked with proving that my brain works outside of being in a constant dream, the Christians should be tasked with proving that I'm not really their god in bodily form just testing their faith by professing Atheism.

Finally, I must point out that Christians and Atheists alike all agree that we *have* brains and senses, and the existence of those are not in dispute. Senses can be thoroughly tested, and yield similar if not exact results in many different environments. The Christian god does not stand up to those tests—no god does. Dr. Creamer once asked me *"Have you ever seen a puddle on a dry road? Once I answered yes, he laughed and said "Then you can't trust your senses."* Well, if I should throw out my knowledge in vision because it lets me down once in a while, Christians should have thrown out the possibility of a god after the second or third child was molested, or the thousandth prayer wasn't answered. Besides, my sense of vision is also what corrected the information and let me know that the puddle wasn't really there. Again, Christians can't say the same for their god. This argument just doesn't work.

The next comment I absolutely had to address was by a caller named Alicia, who offered the conundrum that I've dealt with since age sixteen. But she asked it with such confidence and seriousness that it needed to be addressed on the air. *"There are two possible scenarios in the end. Is it worth taking the chance to not believe?"* As the radio host pointed out, this is commonly known as 'Pascal's Wager.' The common point is that it's just safer to toe the line and believe than to be Atheist, only to find out you're wrong and suffer eternal punishment.

Forgive my candor, but I must admit this is one of the weaker arguments for any religion to make. One could easily counter that with "Then why aren't you Jewish?" The point is, just believing in *something* isn't the path to eternal happiness, and if you're just going through the motions as a safety net, that's not true *belief* anyway, and you're in the same boat I'm in but afraid to admit it. Besides, I don't personally feel like belief is a choice. I can only believe that which makes sense to me, and if I can't make myself believe it, I can't help that anymore than you could force yourself to believe in Santa Clause again. If you don't think it's really there, you can't help that. That's not a choice. To top it off, it's utterly ridiculous to think you could fool an all-knowing being by having a *belief* just to be safe from punishment.

Casey was next up as she quoted Jeremiah 29, which says "seek and you shall find" and she followed that by saying *"David Smalley needs to experience it for himself."* I responded by saying that I actually couldn't agree more! The only hole in the logic there is if I never 'find' anything, I will just be accused of not 'seeking' correctly! If I say that I've 'sought' for several years and finally discovered Atheism, they respond by saying I found the devil instead, or that I need to keep looking. As long as magic is involved, I can't win that one. To bring the reader around to my struggle with this logic, I can only offer an analogy I once used in a speech:

Let's say I took you and 35 friends to a wide open field that was miles wide and miles long and said that somewhere in the field there was an ancient gold coin on the ground worth $100 Million. All you had to do was find it, and it was yours. Of course you would begin looking, but how long would you continue? At the beginning, there's not a lot of cost involved, because it only takes a few minutes to walk around and look. But after a few hours, days, weeks, or months, you might come to me and begin to question the validity of what I've told you, or ask for hints or more guidance. Each time you came to me complaining with your doubts, I could simply respond with, "Maybe you're not looking correctly" or "maybe you misunderstood my instructions." And when someone finally stands up to me and says, "I don't believe a coin is even out here!" I could simply respond with, "Prove it," placing the nearly impossible task of proving my monumental claim to be negative back on the person I have told the story to in the first place. In this analogy, the Atheists are the ones that go home first. They've had enough, and it's not worth it, considering there is no empirical evidence to prove the journey to be worthwhile. This one seemed to sink in, and I think it resulted in many of the listeners understanding the Atheist perspective.

I then had to address one of the more emotional callers who felt an amazing connection with her lord. Her name was Eva, and she said, *"I work as a nurse, and I often pray to God during my shift for guidance and to have more compassion for my patients."* As I stated before, I do have an appreciation for prayer when it's done to look for answers or to ask for strength. I really do think that prayer works, just not for the same reason the theists do. I simply responded by saying that when Eva goes to pray, she's simply talking to herself and tapping into her conscience for what to do next in hard situations. We all do that, and it doesn't require belief in a god to think things through. The answer she receives is from her own brain and her own experiences and her own education, training, and compassion, that is already within her. I cannot prove a metaphysical power isn't helping her any more than she can prove it is. I can only say that Atheists work through issues like that all the time without the assumption of any god or higher guidance. We think, we talk aloud, we work through problems and we do just fine.

The next two questions were posed by Gary, the caller who nearly received the Stump-the-Atheist award, for his well thought-out questions! He said, *"DNA is an information source. All information we know of comes from a designer. What reason can an Atheist give me for how DNA began without a designer?"* My quick and easy answer was, "Every designer we've known to exist has been born, so who are the parents of the designer you're speaking of?" He would have to say, "My god always existed," and I would have to say, "We do not yet know when or where the origin of life took place, but we're getting closer to answering that question." At some point, we are both making an assumption. His just has its source in magic and metaphysical powers, while my assumption is that one day we will know when life originated through the study of science. Nonetheless, it was a great question.

Gary also posed this to me: *"As an Atheistic materialist, if chemicals are all that we are, then we have no choice for what we believe."* Dr. Wooddell added that an Atheistic materialist would hold the belief that our brain chemicals cannot be controlled, therefore it must be predetermined by our brain matter for what our beliefs will be. These both take some deep thought to respond to if we choose to defend them, and questions like these are the reasons why Atheists tend to not make specific claims as religions do in a pretentious notion that we have all knowledge of the universe, or are at least close to the man that does. The Atheist doesn't make a claim that needs to be defended. Our primary statement is that theistic beliefs are without sufficient proof. When we say that, and the Christian or Muslim or Jew responds with "then prove my god isn't real," we end up back to my *coin in the field* analogy where no one can win as long as there's mystery and faith.

But to answer the man's question of chemicals versus choices, I offered the fact presented in biologist Frank R. Zindler's 1985 essay "Spirit, Soul, and Mind," that states 'mind' is a process, not a thing. Yes we have thoughts, but those thoughts are a result of chemical responses to stimuli, just as decisions are made based on interests, value, and perception. I don't see myself as a hard determinist, and I'm certainly not one who holds the position that anything is 'predetermined.' But as I stated before, I do not think belief is a choice. When facts are presented to our eyes as a stimulus that results in a chemical response (which coupled with experience from previous knowledge), this allows us to make a decision, and therefore the process of *mind* takes place. We can't fool ourselves into a belief we don't agree with. So in a way, the caller is right, we don't really have a choice to be Atheist or Christian, but it has nothing to do with determinism—only the way we interpret the facts presented to us and the way our chemicals produce a process of response. Things like love, hope, desire, nervousness, and fear, are processes of chemical stimuli but are not decisions or choices we have made. It is obvious that chemicals can change, and it's obvious that believers sometimes become nonbelievers, and *vice-versa*. One only needs to look into the lives of C.S. Lewis and Lee Strobel for one example, and to Dan Barker and Charles Templeton for the other. This just means that different stimuli mean different things for all of us, and until it makes sense to us, we can't force ourselves to believe it. That's where I've been for the last thirteen years and counting. I can't *make it* make sense.

Regardless of how anyone chooses to rip apart my arguments or explanations above with opposing views, or say that I don't have enough evidence for 'Atheism,' you must remember that this doesn't get us any closer to proving that Christianity is the one true belief system or that Yahweh is the one true god. That's why Atheism is not a religion. There is nothing to prove, there is no doctrine, there are no inspired books of rules; but only questions to be asked by those that claim to have all those answers in the form of magic and personal relationships with unknown spirits.

The final comment I needed to respond to was by the host himself, Dr. Barry Creamer. When I challenged the problem of evil and mentioned the children in Haiti that were devastated by the earthquake in 2010, he used the analogy of going to the dentist to get a shot before pulling a tooth. His purpose was that the shot causes pain and suffering, which is therefore evil, but is necessary in the long run to pull the tooth. Once again, an inaccurate analogy is being made. The one major difference is this: The shot is *necessary* to prevent further pain of pulling the tooth. The earthquake is *not necessary* to have eternal happiness in Christianity, and I challenge the reader to find any legitimate Christian doctrine that says otherwise.

I enjoyed my time speaking with the folks on *Live From Criswell*, and hope I gave their listeners a lot to think about. From the looks of the comments on my blog, I absolutely did! Several comments have poured in from listeners challenging my position on multiple levels but also asking questions. I've also received a few of those anonymous emails saying *"don't tell anyone, but I've always agreed those things too."* I was just hoping that I too, could spark someone's journey. Perhaps I have.

# CHAPTER 7: LIFE AFTER THE JOURNEY

## SECULAR HUMANISM

Confirming your Atheism only means you have chosen to base your life on honesty, reason, and helping people in need because they need it, not because a religion demands it. As an Atheist, you trust provable and testable theories of scientific evidence as opposed to a mythical spiritual beginning of man. An Atheist asserts that it is better to perform a single good deed from the kindness of one's heart than for a thousand lips to pray to a god.

The Secular Humanists love and help our fellow man and do everything in their power to have a positive influence on someone, or the planet. We do our best to make a difference while we're here. We do not unjustly murder, commit rape, or steal. We feel that each person should be held responsible for his or her actions on Earth, and what laws you break on Earth shall be punished on Earth, so that no one should escape into death. We treat one another with the same respect and dignity we demand for ourselves. We honor our family and history through cultural dignity and ethical standards in society. We obey laws and do not feel that any metaphysical being supersedes those laws. We are each responsible for our own actions and problem solving. We do not place things 'in the hands of a god,' but instead, we drive our own destiny. These are simply natural, materialistic world views, not a specific system of beliefs that an Atheist 'must' follow. There are no rituals, no chants, no scripts, and no sacrifices. That is left to religion. The most beautiful part about this, is if we ever found evidence that showed that any of these were not the best practices for our society, we would abandon them at once and reevaluate our entire situation. Religionists are not willing to do that. They are not willing to improve. If the lifestyle is uncomfortable, it is the *believer* that is the problem, because the religion is viewed as perfect.

With these definitions of life and ethics in mind, I want to make it clear that being an Atheist basically means you have a scientific difference of opinion as it pertains to the creation of life and other metaphysical claims. It does not mean your values are less, or you are less of a person. If you do not truly feel that the evidence points to the existence of a spirit, or that a god created you at all, you cannot help that. *Atheism isn't a choice, it's a realization.* The only way you can be religious at that point is to lie to yourself, and that's not healthy or promoted in any religion or belief. Remember, it was a pastor who began my journey toward Atheism by uttering the phrase, *"You have to know it to be true in your heart."*

Atheists are a disrespected minority, and if you come to the realizations of Atheism, you are then representing all of us each time you discuss religion. If you are Atheist, please be mindful of that, and please try not to become hateful or insulting during a conversation. Religion is a sensitive topic for many people, and in my opinion, you should only discuss it for the purposes of correcting religious wrongs, matters of civil rights, education, exploring human culture, or rescuing dishonest Atheists from their beliefs which have them trapped. Attacking religionists for the purpose of mockery doesn't do any of us any good.

I recommend that you educate yourself but not be arrogant in your ways of disagreeing. I am guilty of this myself sometimes, because it's hard to be nice in a fight. But we have to understand that as Atheists, we do not believe. Therefore, if someone says that the Christian god *does* exist, it shouldn't offend us. On the other hand, when an Atheist says the Christian god *does not* exist, he or she is saying that every preacher, pastor, nun, and pope, has lived a life in a certain way, worshiping nothing, and paying homage to a fictitious being. That can obviously be offensive.

So what's the point in an organized Atheist group? The primary focus of organized Atheists is to offer help and love to fellow man instead of gods. In addition, we strive to uphold the constitutional right of separating church and state and to prevent religion from being forced down the throats of society—especially those of our children in public schools. Our country was based on freedom of thought and civil liberties of all citizens.

## THE OTHER CLOSET

Many people who finally realize the odds are greatly stacked against the Christian god's existence often ask themselves the question, "What now?" "What's the purpose of life, and why should I care, if there is no holy afterlife to look forward to?" Those are legitimate questions. However, for Atheists, the answer is the same: peace and solidarity within the truth. You are now working to experience a paradise on earth as opposed to waiting until after death. Whatever brings you happiness within the limits of the law, and our standard sociological and ethical set of behavior, is what you should make of your life-long goals. You no longer need to waste time chasing hopes of perfection or attempting to abide by impossible rules. You are free—free from guilt, free from demons, free from being watched, and free from a fear of eternal punishment. You no longer need to live a life riddled with guilt for each impure thought you may have. You no longer need to live in fear of any god or demonic spirit. You should no longer feel as if you are imperfect or not good enough. Your new life focus can be on your happiness and success as well as that of your family. You should strive to learn more about man, as you have learned about the Christian god in the past. Discovering more about yourself, and your own species, will only make you closer to those around you and allow a greater acceptance of who you are and who you want to be.

However, this decision will not come without some heartache. Many people realize they do not believe in their family's religion, but few speak up and take a stand. The majority of Atheists or other non-believers either don't want to upset the family or just don't care enough to fight for it, but either way, there are more closet Atheists than you could shake a stick at, and I hear from them on a daily basis in the form of anonymous emails and blog posts.

Trust me; I understand what they are going through. At a time when most mothers would be extremely proud of their son's completed education and the publishing of his first book, I was being told that my immediate family was no longer welcome to the holiday celebrations. What did I do to deserve this? I simply spoke up. I passed out Winter Solstice cards one year at a Christmas party, educating others in my family of the original ancient celebrations to give them a good understanding of why we don't celebrate for the same reasons they do. The following year, I was told to never come back for that celebration. The family views it as though I've changed, when in reality, *Christmas* is the new celebration, and the Winter Solstice was there long before any myths were added. I simply discovered that fact and tried to share the truth with my loved ones. This was a divisive moment in my family's history, but we have since made a general compromise and a non-religious celebration for everyone who chooses to attend.

Even with this semi-compromise that is still evolving at the time of writing, the tension is clear. In fact, as I gained ground and popularity through my blogs, videos, magazines, and multiple radio appearances, all in an attempt to protect the civil rights of all Americans, my mother didn't stop to think about the wonderful good that could come from this. She didn't consider the many fights in the family that would be non-existent if religious claims were ignored, or if I wasn't discriminated against in the work force, what more I could accomplish. She didn't think to rationalize the laws I could overturn that currently violate my rights by prohibiting me from serving in public office because I lack a 'belief in the Creator,' which is on the books of several states in our country. When hearing public figures talk about me so much, I never once heard that she was proud of my activism, authorship, education, or popularity. She could only utter the phrase *"I wish they would stop using your last name."*

As I previously stated, Matthew 10:34–35 has Jesus saying that he did not come to bring peace, but division; to set a man against his father, and a daughter against her mother. He may have never existed, that I am unsure of. But at least in my lifetime, his legacy has been successful in doing just that, at least temporarily, in my family. But realistically, I understand that I can't fully blame my mother, or other family members for distancing themselves from me. It is so ingrained, and hammered into us that it becomes very real and very scary to let go of. I can only hope that someday they will take the journey I have taken and see religion for what it is. But I am not the only one with this problem.

I received a letter from a listener who struggled as a closet Atheist. Here are some excerpts from his writing—perhaps you can relate:

*Dear David,*

*I recently heard your radio show on Atheism and I think you did an excellent job of telling your story and analyzing the Bible and the concept of God. I am an African American man living in the South, so you can imagine that I was raised in a religious (Baptist) household. I was forced to go to church as a child... I could never figure out why I didn't feel these spiritual feelings that other folks have.*

*I'm 41 now, but most of my adult life (going back as far as age 14) I struggled with believing in the existence of God. I had so many questions, even at that early age. Why did God stop talking to us (verbally)?...Why do we have to have a Hell?*

*My mother, knowing I had these questions, would set up meetings with myself and the pastor and he would always point to scriptures to explain all of my questions. That wasn't enough for me because the Bible is a book.*

*I guess if I had to label myself, I would say that I am more of a "closet Atheist." I don't publicly tell anyone that I question the existence of God because people FREAK OUT and get hysterical. They cannot handle a mere discussion about the possibility of there being no God. They think that they are getting a one-way ticket to Hell just for having the discussion... Many of them get angry and furious and tell me that I am going to suffer damnation in Hell.*

*I will continue to remain anonymous and I don't tell anyone my true questions and beliefs...I will also keep checking your page for more material from you. I look forward to it."*

My reply:

*Anonymous,*

*Thank you very much for your comments, and thanks for writing! We've all been in a bad relationship, where we struggle to make things work, thinking we can force happiness—and it never comes. Then one day, we find that special someone and suddenly realize, while some work is always needed, it's such a relief to love someone you believe in!*

*Well, religion and free thought have a similar relationship. For a while, I was a bit of a closet Atheist myself, until I started reading material other Atheists had written. It felt so refreshing to finally read something that made sense, instead of trying to force nonsense to work out rationally. What a relief it was to read an Atheist write his thoughts or clearly state his case in a debate! I no longer felt alone.*

*Once I finally felt at home and at peace with being an Atheist (first trying to get over the bad taste that word left in my mouth due to years of sociological brainwashing) I began to feel this awesome lift of burdens leaving me that could never return. I have no more guilt for being born. I have no more sinning qualities. My ethics are humanistic principles, and I've never been happier! That is a joy that I cannot explain. Seeing that type of freedom enrages those of faith, because they don't understand how you can have love, peace, happiness, and be successful without ever praying or sacrificing.*

*To an Atheist, this new lifestyle brings confidence and contentment. It frees up so much time to do work for others and help those in need. The true humanist can come out once you're no longer afraid of gods, or preachers, or church societies that may judge you. You're not asking "What Would Jesus Do?" you're asking someone less fortunate, "What do you need ME to do?"*

*Looking at religions objectively, you finally realize the worshipper's life is based on hiding how they really feel, hiding the things they really do, making excuses for their 'sinful' actions, and being too afraid to face the possibility of being alone in this universe. Once you accept those as facts, and no longer fear them, you have an amazing power to be you. You no longer have to live by some conjured up 'moral code,' and your instincts can be set free.*

*In time, I hope your Atheism shines through and will eventually lead you to a life of Humanism and secular giving and volunteering. Regardless of where your beliefs or non-beliefs take you, please continue your research.*

*I recommend first and foremost, reading the Bible. Seriously. An objective ethical look into the Bible was the primary cause of my Atheism. Also, read* Atheism Advanced *by Dr. David Eller (available at atheists.org). I'm just finishing that up and it has been amazing! Also, to stay current on lawsuits and the latest battles facing Atheists of our time, I of course have to recommend subscribing to the* American Atheist *magazine, of which I am so proudly the editor! (Also available at atheists.org.)*

*And if this research leads you to Christianity, or any other religion—then so be it! At the end of the day, the important thing is finding that way of life that allows you to be comfortable in your own skin. Whether you're homosexual, Muslim, Christian, or Atheist, the closet is no place to live.*

*I hope to hear from you again. Feel free to anonymously post any questions you may have on my Web-site, as I would love to chat. Keep thinking, and start debating.*

*—David*

Customarily, when people are baptized, they embark on an incredible journey and try their best to walk in the footsteps of Jesus. I too did the same thing, but I may have walked that journey a little too carefully, and analyzed that text a little too closely. I paid a little too much attention.

As I've stated before, an Atheist is not someone who knows too little about Christianity, but he or she is often one that has studied too many religions, and asked too many questions. It is a bit ironic that the very moment I was baptized into the Christian faith was also the moment that was the catalyst that led to my Atheism. I wanted to be 'closer to God,' but I got so close that I could see he wasn't there. It was all a result of my baptism. In a sense, I was probably the world's first *Baptized Atheist*.

# THINGS TO PONDER
## QUOTES BY DAVID SMALLEY

*"You will not have the opportunity to make a difference after death, so be someone's guardian angel now."*

*"Just as religions can take a simple man and make him godly, it can also take a great man and make him evil."*

*"Some people feel they need religion because they can't control themselves; but it shouldn't be forced upon those of us who can."*

*"Just as funerals are for the living, not the dead; religions are for the people, not the gods."*

*"If we truly had one creator speaking to prophets, it would do so consistently, not contradictorily as thousands of different religions have proven."*

*"If the Christian god created humans as sinners, how could it rightfully expect us to believe its corrupt messengers?"*

*"Let us find our own answers
and make an educated decision,
rather than remaining uneducated
and making a fearful one."*

*"If the holy books were truly
such, and inspired by omniscient
beings, they would not be limited to
the knowledge of those who wrote them."*

*"It is a complete contradiction to say
that a righteous god would purposely
create you imperfectly, and then expect
you to begin an impossible race to
perfection before death."*

*"We have the capacity to make
decisions based on value and
reason instead of hope and fear."*

*"If it is impossible for you
to choose the same sex against your
will, don't you think it's impossible
for homosexuals to choose the opposite?"*

*"I was a believer too; and I must
tell you, my sense of the urgency of
life is ten-fold greater now that
I no longer believe in Heaven."*

*"Those who place their lives and
hardships in the hands of a god
are those who have given
up on themselves."*

# SPECIAL THANKS

I must offer my greatest respect and thanks to my daughter Talissa, and to my son Brayden, for putting up with my long hours working on this project and the many years I dedicated to research and education in a quest for knowledge of psychology and religion. The few times I skipped family outings, dinners, or play time, I truly wanted to be there, but had a commitment to myself and to you to finish this.

Kids, I often heard you playing just outside the window and wanted so badly to join you! Although we still had our good times, and I occasionally made my way out there to chase you around, and jump the ramps on a bicycle as if I were ten years old again, I know there could have been more. I want you to learn from this, that some level of sacrifice is necessary for true success. I just wanted to be able to provide you with the truth, and I couldn't do that until I had the truth myself. Thank you for understanding, and get ready for a lot more play time!

I must also single out Mr. Frank R. Zindler, whose transcript online regarding the radio debate of Noah's Flood sparked my activism in Atheism, and for that, I can rightfully credit this book. His inspiration, long hours, and activism through rough times are something I will always hold in high regard. I am very thankful for the support of everyone at the American Atheists organization, and I credit Mr. Zindler with assisting in the discovery of my identity.

Thank you also, to the rest of my family for all the debates. Your ideas about religion were a great insight into the way Americans generally think about religious life, and I was able to address that accordingly, as you were an excellent window into reality, and America's perception of religion and Atheists. This book was written for you. I sincerely hope you forgive my candor and appreciate my tone.

Finally, I must encourage those who are inspired my writing to continue the activism. So many people simply make fun of religions, or mock them in a vulgar way that is detrimental to our success in the movement. Please don't be one of those. Remain respectful—for it's only those that  have ran out of things to say that feel they must resort to name-calling. We have plenty to say. Say it loudly. Say it proudly. And always stand up against that which you do not believe in.

# ABOUT THE AUTHOR

David Smalley is the Editor of the *American Atheist: A Journal of Atheist News and Thought.* The national magazine is the flagship publication of American Atheists, Inc. and focuses on news and opinions concerning Atheists—especially those in the movement to maintain the separation of church and state and protect the rights of non-religious Americans.

Mr. Smalley has written more than one-hundred articles and blogs on various topics concerning Atheism, and is also the host and moderator of the popular religious discussion site, "The Dogma Debate." (www.dogmadebate.com)

He has been heard on Dallas radio—90.9 FM KCBI, 570 AM KLIF, 1360 KMNY, 910 AM KATH, EWTN Global Catholic radio, and 1400 AM KREF in Oklahoma, discussing various topics on religion and Atheism.

David co-hosts *The Dogma Debate* radio show with his partner, Todd Hyso, from a perspective unique to David's education in psychology, and dedication to helping those in need.

# REFERENCES

**Baumeister, Roy.,** (2001). Evil: Inside Human Violence and Cruelty. New York: Barnes & Noble Books.

**Columbia University:** Bible Canonization retrieved: Thurs. 3/4/2010. http://www.columbia.edu/cu/augustine/arch/sbrandt/nicea.htm

**Dawkins, Richard.,** (2009). *The Greatest Show on Earth: the evidence for evolution.* Free Press. 1230 Avenue of the Americas, New York, NY 10020

**Eller, David.,** (2007). *Atheism Advanced, Further Thoughts of a Freethinker.* American Atheist Press, Cranford, New Jersey.

**Freud, Sigmund.,** (1921). Group Psychology and the Analysis of the Ego. James Strachey, trans. New York: Bantam Books.

**Holy Bible,** King James Version

**Horn, Geoffrey., & Cavanaugh, Arthur.,** (1980). *Bible Stories for Children.* Abraham, 34–39

**Hitchens, Christopher.,** (2007). *God is not great : how religion poisons everything.* Allen & Unwin, Crows Nest, N.S.W.

**Hubble, Edwin.,** (1929). *A Relation between Distance and Radial Velocity among Extra-Galactic Nebulae.* Proceedings of the National Academy of Science. USA 15, 168–173

**Klaczynski, P.A.,** (2001). *Analytic and heuristic processing influences on adolescent reasoning and decision-making.* Child Development, 72, 844–861.

**Robinson-Riegler, C., & Robinson Riegler, B.** (2008). *Cognitive Psychology: Applying the science of the mind.* Reasoning, Judgment and Decision Making. p 485-531.

**Sheldon, William.**, (1949). Varieties of Delinquent Youth. New York: Harper & Row.

**Templeton, Charles.**, (1996). *Farwell to God: My Reasons For Rejecting the Christian Faith.* Noah and the Great Flood. McClelland & Stewart: Toronto, Ontario.

**Thiroux, J., & Krasemann, K.**, (2009) *Ethics: Theory and Practice* Tenth Edition, pp. 21., Custom Publishing, New York

**Winfree, L. T. & Abadinsky, H.**, (2003). Understanding Crime: Theory andPractice, Second Edition. Belmont, California: Wadsworth/Thomson Learning.

**World Resources Institute:** http://www.wri.org/publication/content/8202

**Zindler, Frank R.**, (1985). "Spirit, Soul, and Mind" *American Atheist:* American Atheist Press, Cranford, New Jersey.